MW01170718

Thank you for not talking

A Laughable Look at Introverts

BEN ALPER

ISBN-13: 978-0-578-48216-3

Editing by Bill Bowers and Joyce Alper
Cover design by Lucy Bartholomay
Book design by Classic GraphX

First Printing edition

www.bennettalper.com
Bennett.Alper@gmail.com

To Monica

Contents

4. Small Talk: One Tiny Sentence for Man, One Agonizing Moment for Introverts 32

5. Stuck Inside Your Head: I Had Me at Hello 38

6. Why Are You So Quiet? A Babbling World Wants to Know 43

Introduction

Introverts, rejoice! Once we were lonely, alienated, frustrated souls trapped inside our thoughts. Thanks to an onslaught of enlightened books and blogs, we are now awesome. We get the big picture. We have amazing friends. We're desirable as mates. To think we would've been satisfied just to make it to our mailboxes without bumping into an overly chatty neighbor.

We are living the dream in our rent-free heads. The best part? If we feel cramped, we can always imagine a bigger head.

There are all kinds of introverts, from people who occasionally need some time alone to those who haven't left their apartments since the Carter administration.

Regardless of where you sit on the silent spectrum, you will enjoy reading this book if you are:

An extreme introvert who relishes lively debates with yourself about philosophy, politics, and art.

A moderate introvert who savors the company of close friends but also craves an occasional solitary Netflix binge with a bag of potato chips and a gallon of Ben & Jerry's.

A mild introvert who is comfortable with small talk in large crowds but begins to falter slightly after the tenth "I'm a semi-retired party balloon inflator. What do you do for a living?"

Even an extrovert who can't refrain from tapping an introvert's head and asking if they're up for an intimate party of 20,000 at Madison Square Garden.

This book does not sing the praises of introverts. It does not explain how to have mind-blowing introvert sex. It doesn't even include five easy steps to better eye contact. This comedy-writing author simply takes a funny look at the way introverts are, as he's always known them to be.

Note: If your goal is to become the world's best introvert or convert to extroversion, please refer to any book with a title ending in "for Dummies." For the rest of you, find a quiet, peaceful place to read and enjoy! I recommend a tastefully decorated isolation tank.

CHAPTER 1

Who Are Introverts and Why Don't They High-Five?

An introvert is someone who is easily drained by social interaction. It could be with anyone, but especially with obnoxious workmates, pushy realtors, and Brazilian wax technicians.

Being alone recharges introverts, as opposed to extroverts, who are energized by talking the FedEx guy's head off.

Twenty-five percent of the world is introverted. This number could actually be greater because we don't know how many Dinka tribesmen hate going to crowded fertility rituals.

There are different levels of introversion. They range from people who can't survive a sales meeting without medical attention to folks who haven't spoken to another human since the Surgeon General declared smoking cigarettes cured acne.

Introverts actually enjoy social interaction, but with small groups of people with whom we have deep, insightful conversation—for example, debating why mustaches grow down instead of up. Small talk is difficult, but we enjoy intense conversation. You don't see a lot of introverts hawking beer at football stadiums, except the ones who enjoy explaining to fans the brewing process in Lithuania.

Another Introvert Sighting

Another introvert was recently sighted at a local beach. The lone figure appeared briefly for twelve hours, during which time scientists were able to attach an electronic tracking device. The subject, whom they designated "Bob" exhibits several classic introvert personality traits.

- Even after being introduced to the group of fourteen observers, he refuses to join the scientists in their daily group hug.

- Being with people for extended periods of time drains him of energy—especially when being held down while someone attaches a monitoring device to his ankle.

- He is very self-aware. The scientists theorize it's because he's been obsessing about himself for the past twenty years.

- He always thinks a long time before talking, which makes him a very thoughtful person, except when reporting swimmers in distress.

- Too much stimulation leaves him feeling distracted and unfocused. After foreplay, he can never remember why he took his pants off.

- He often feels alone in a crowd. This is why he always brings a book to read at flash mobs.

- It's easy for him to give a speech to 500 people but harder to mingle with them after. Fortunately, he has perfected his "Excuse me, I have to go feed my hamster" line.

Ask Mindy Menorah:

My Kid Won't Say the Darndest Things . . . or Anything Else

Dear Mindy: Our son is an extreme introvert. He has just a few friends, most of whom are imaginary and not particularly friendly. He stays in his room most of the time. We have to practically beg him to join our family's weekly Slovakian trivia night.

Things had gotten so bad we had no choice but to hire a highly regarded introvert deprogrammer (he has his own Instagram page), who kidnapped him and kept him at his private institute in the Poconos for two weeks. The results were disastrous. Our son spent most of the time taking solitary walks in the woods and having deep philosophical discussions with the other introverts. He returned unchanged. In fact, our son wants to return to the Poconos next summer for a "spiritual renewal" with his new reclusive friends.

Where did we go wrong?
Flummoxed in Flicksville

Dear Flummoxed: Introversion is not a condition that can be treated like a fear of Belgian waffles. Although you may never understand your son's introvert ways, you need to show him that you love him. Promising not to have him kidnapped and held against again his will is a good start. Also, share an activity that he enjoys, like sitting alone in your bedrooms. Does your employer celebrate Take Your Introvert to Work Day? It's a great way for your child to observe your world and then flee after five minutes.

Mindy Menorah, Ph.D., LCSW, AWOL *is a licensed, bonded, and bounded couples therapist. For twenty-three years she was the official Osmond family mediator.*

Great Things about Being an Introvert

HAPPY
introvert

- You're very self-aware of things like the sound of hair growing out of your head.

- You're not a snob; you just have a hard time connecting with the lesser people beneath you.

- You're creative. You can think of countless ways to say, "Why are you charging me for HBO and Showtime?"

Not-So-Great Things about Being an Introvert

SAD
introvert

- People always ask, "Why aren't you talking?" Particularly the person who hired you as an auctioneer.

- Coworkers assume you don't like them, just because you do your best work while sitting in a restroom stall.

- It's hard to arouse another person sexually with a cynical stare.

Archeologists Discover Paleolithic Introvert

A team of archaeologists excavating an ancient apothecary under a CVS in Roanoke, Virginia discovered the remains of the world's oldest known introvert. Scientists called the 130,000-year-old female skeleton *Homo standoffish* and nicknamed her Alma. She differed drastically from other humans of this era, providing a glimpse into the early age of introversion.

Alma preferred staying in her cave alone and reading wall paintings. She rarely socialized with other *Homo sapiens*. When she did, she preferred long, intense conversations about not being killed by a large animal.

She occasionally attended fertility rituals and human sacrifices but fled large gatherings after a short time to "recharge."

Since the average vocabulary of her time was limited to three or four grunts, small talk was problematic for Alma. Most party talk consisted of "How do you know the host?" and "I thought the host had been eaten by a lion."

Alma had a rich inner life, and was the first known creature to obsess on two legs.

Like most introverts, Alma never felt comfortable being the center of attention. She had good reason to feel that way after finding herself surrounded by a neighboring tribe who overreacted to her satiric cave mural, "Toothless Fools." Fortunately, she died of old age before the horde could sacrifice her to no one in particular.

Ask Dr. Introvert

Question	Answer
Why are introverts so quiet?	Introverts are often consumed with deep and profound thoughts like "How can mankind sustain itself?" or "Should I order pepperoni or sausage pizza?"
Are all introverts sensitive?	No, but most are. In fact, seventy-three percent can detect when their pet turtle is having a severe mood shift.
Do introverts hate people?	No. Many regularly reach out to strangers by filing warm and inviting restraining orders.
Does a person's upbringing affect whether they will be an introvert?	Only if their parents named them Appaloosa, Draven, or Little Sweetmeat.
Why do introverts dislike small talk?	They enjoy deeper conversation. Why say "I like music" when you can recite the entire iTunes user agreement?
Can drugs change an introvert into an extrovert?	No, but with enough medication some introverts are able to tell a sweating stranger on a hot, crowded bus to seriously consider deodorant.

Dr. Introvert *(not his real name) is a board-certified psychologist who treats patients suffering from fear of itchy underwear. He also holds numerous medical instrument patents including one for stereophonic heart resuscitation paddles.*

Introvert Hall of Fame Inductees Announced

Introvert Hall of Fame executive director Regina Reclusaconti announced this year's inductees. Some notable honorees include:

Helen "Muffin" English: Longtime White House correspondent English never asked a question for thirty-two years until her final day, when she demanded to know the location of the ladies' room.

Thelma Anne Louise: J.C. Penny employee Louise is the only cashier in history to process over a million sales transactions without engaging a customer in trivial conversation. The closest she came to idle chatter was in 1968, when she told a shopper, "Your fly is down."

Ernie "Frozen Call" Dawkins: In an unintentional groundbreaking experiment, telemarketer Dawkins proved that staring at a phone while in a cold sweat for eight hours a day is not conducive to selling vinyl siding.

Cecil "Sweaty Palms" Singletary: Dating maven Singletary has driven over 100,000 miles around city blocks to avoid arriving at singles mixers early. His circular travels also earned him an inadvertent induction into the Stalkers Hall of Fame.

Ilia Onandon: NPR talk show host Onandon has interviewed one guest since 1985: himself. Few will forget his 2003 Valentine's Day discussion, in which he proposed to his inner voice and was rejected.

At the honorees' request, the formal induction will be conducted by registered mail.

Introvert Myths

Google the word "introvert" and you'll find countless websites waxing poetic about us moody wonders. Are we quiet, spiritual souls or personality-deficient party poopers? The truth lies somewhere in between. The following clarifies a few introvert myths.

Myth	Reality
We are quiet because we always think about deep and spiritual things.	Some introverts are still wondering if a Walmart cashier shortchanged them in 2003.
We hate small talk because it bores us.	Some introverts you meet at a party are actually interested in what you do for a living—if you're preparing to flee the country to avoid embezzlement charges.
We are great writers.	Some introverts can only write home for money.
Introverts hate being in crowds.	Some introverts like to rub gently against passengers on crowded buses and subways.
Human interaction exhausts us.	Some introverts are too ashamed to admit they love binge watching TV while eating junk food.
We are good at seeing the big picture.	Some introverts think the big picture involves secret government control of our toothpaste reserves.
We have a constant, rich, and fascinating inner monologue.	Some introverts can bore even themselves.
We are very sensitive people.	Some introverts will ask you to pass the ketchup while you announce you're a cocker spaniel trapped in a woman's body.
We intrigue people.	Some introverts scare people.

Do You Feel Like an Invisible Introvert?

We introverts can feel invisible in a chattering world of gabbers. You might not recognize the feeling at first, but the signs are always there.

- Whenever you ask a question in class, your teacher responds, "Yes, the chair in the back."
- Your retirement watch has been engraved "The Guy in Cubicle 35-B."
- The only one at the party aware of your presence is a floor lamp with whom you are dissecting China trade policy.
- During sex your partner screams her own name.
- In high school, you were voted *Most Likely to Pass Through Airport Security X-ray Machines Undetected*.
- The voices in your head talk as if you're not there.
- The drunk you've been subtly flashing your cleavage at keeps asking a bowl of peanuts for its phone number.

Unfortunately, invisibility isn't there when you need it. Think about that the next time your workmates corner you in the lunchroom with a birthday cake.

World's Oldest Introvert Dies

Camila Montalban, the world's oldest introvert, has died in Bel Air, California. She passed away at the age of 118 while doing what she loved best, staring quietly out the window.

Montalban, who attributed her longevity to sleep, eating healthy food alone, and never revealing her address to countless relatives and nosey neighbors, died at 10:38 a.m. Wednesday. She collapsed while listening to a Meals on Wheels deliveryman drone on endlessly about Styrofoam containers and never regained consciousness.

Camila was born on August 2, 1899 in San Diego, California. Her father was a Maytag washboard repairman. Her mother was a part-time Greco-Roman wrestler. She didn't speak her first word until age twelve, later explaining, "I didn't have anything to say."

When not pretending to listen to her husband and children, she enjoyed rehashing arguments in her head and anxiously waiting for parties to end. A history buff, Camilla founded a club that researched and reenacted famous moments of silence.

With Camila Montalban's death, the title of world's oldest introvert now belongs to Takeo Fukuda, a 112-year-old World War II Japanese soldier who refused to surrender because he preferred the quiet and slow pace of jungle living.

CHAPTER 2

Are You an Introvert or Are You Just Nervous to See Me?

How do you know if you're an introvert? The fact you're reading this book is a tipoff.

Did you throw this book at a friend who gave it to you? That's another tipoff—especially if she gave it to you at your surprise birthday you begged her not to throw.

Regardless how you feel, read this chapter. It never hurts to get another opinion beyond a personality test in *Cat Lovers* Magazine.

Ten Signs You Are an Introvert

1. You are constantly texting the voice in your head.

2. You often feel alone in a mosh pit.

3. Small talk is agony but small talk with a talkative small person is torture.

4. When attending public events, you always sit in the back row, even if it's on someone's lap.

5. You notice details others don't. For example, you're the only earthling on your condo board.

6. It's hard to make small foreplay at orgies.

7. People keep telling you to "say something," particularly during debating competitions.

8. You often get lost in your thoughts. In fact, your mind has drifted and you've stopped reading this.

9. Your favorite exit strategy for fleeing social gatherings is yelling "Fire!" while leaping casually out a window.

10. According to your Myers-Briggs Type Indicator assessment, you're an observer, best suited for a career as a peeping tom.

NFL Prospect Announces He's an Introvert

Leon "Sawzall" Sanders, a bruising line-backer for the Alaska State University Salmon, announced Tuesday he is an introvert.

The NFL prospect is poised to become the league's first openly introverted player.

"I understand the implications," he said. "No one has done this before. But if it's going to be me, then so be it . . . hopefully with a minimum of high-fiving and chest bumping."

Sanders said he first suspected he was an introvert in the second grade, when he faked a stomachache to avoid playing Ring Around the Rosie. "People have always assumed I'm aloof, arrogant, and standoffish. Actually, that part is true."

Some experts think Sanders' announcement could lower his selection in the draft. Said an NFL scout, "A lot of players won't like the idea of showering with someone who's not into butt slaps." Added a players' agent, "Most of my clients are conceited, spoiled a-holes, but at least they're friendly when you bail them out of jail. I'm not sure the league is ready for a player who can't fake humility at the ESPY Awards."

The NFL released a statement in support of Sanders: "We admire Leon Sanders' honesty and courage. The league has come a long way since Commissioner Pete Rozelle's infamous and unfortunate observation: 'Johnny Unitas is an unapproachable son of a bitch.'"

Quiet Quiz

There are many signs that indicate whether you are an introvert. For example, are you reading this book instead of attending your wedding reception?

Still not sure? You could be evaluated by a certified Myers-Briggs practitioner, but what if you're too lazy to even Google "Am I an introvert?" No problem. Simply answer these two questions.

Question 1: You are on a train that leaves the station at noon. The train is 187 miles from its destination at 2:45 p.m. and ninety miles from its destination at 4:15 p.m. How far will the train travel before you speak to the passenger sitting next to you?

Question 2: What does this Auguste Rodin's statue, The Thinker, say to you?

1. I'm bored. I think I'll call my friends and see what they're doing.
2. In retrospect, I should've brought a cushion.
3. Finally, I have some time to think.

Calculating your score – If it's not obvious to you by now whether you're an introvert, it may be time to pre-order my forthcoming book, *Plain as the Nose on Your Face*.

I'm Still Here, Reading in My Apartment

One-Woman Show Delivers a Reserved Punch

Judith Andelman reflects on her journey from a single, artistically inclined, withdrawn actress to an unmarried, creative, introverted performer. It's a transformation to behold as she does it while staring at the floor for two and a half hours.

Ms. Andelman—a veteran of countless Off-Off-Off-Broadway productions including "I'm Afraid of Virginia Woolf's Cocktail Parties," The Iceman Cometh and Won't Shut Upeth," and "Rosencrantz and Guildenstern are Boring Me"—explains through music and monologue how she overcame and embraced her introversion.

We watch this gifted, if not approachable, actress blossom before our eyes. As a child sitting in her room, she sings about the joys of solitude ("No One to Watch Over Me"). Her silence is always misinterpreted as standoffishness ("I Go to My Head").

The evening's most heartbreaking moment comes as she hits rock bottom when she is dismissed from a dinner theater production of "A Chorus Line" for insisting she will only dance in the women's restroom. Judith finally realizes "I may have some issues" as she tearfully acknowledges "What I Probably Should Have Done for Love."

Eventually through song and an imaginary therapist, Adelman explores her introversion. This leads to acceptance and self-love. In an emotional finale, she sends the audience home with a heartfelt and inspired "Of Me I Sing (Baby)."

I'm Still Here, Reading in My Apartment: *Created and performed by Judith Andelman; Songs and lyrics by Judith Andelman (pending lawsuits by the estates of George and Ira Gershwin, and many others.)*

Discover Your Inner Introvert

Journey to Your Introverse and Beyond!

Join subconscious spiritual guide, Madame Carma Dioxide, on a divine voyage to your most inner introvert.

The itinerary includes her Sacred-Palooza seminars:

Traveling the Quietly Expressed: Madame Dioxide leads you on a meditative excursion where silence is golden and tipping is optional.

The Zen of Aloneness and Binge Watching: Spend an entire weekend at Madame's astonishingly beautiful Santa Barbara retreat while viewing every episode of *Game of Thrones* season 7 in a sensory deprivation tank (single tanks are extra). Price includes all the frozen pizza and Häagen-Dazs® you can eat.

Toastmasters of the Soul: Learn to trust your inner monologue and better communicate with your unspoken voices. Emphasis on presentation, confidence, and grammar.

Small Talk Survivors Group: Share your experiences with other nonjudgmental survivors in a safe space. Topics include "Beyond 'Nice to meet you'" and "Getting past 'Nice weather we've been having.'"

"Madame Carma Dioxide will lead you to a quiet, tranquil world. She is unquestionably nothingness personified."

—Sixpak Chopra

When Did You Realize You Were an Introvert?

Bob: I remember lying in the hospital nursery thinking, "These crying babies are driving me crazy!" At that moment I realized I was a solitary soul. This also explains why I prefer hysterically crying to playing Trivial Pursuit with more than four people.

Sparky: Don't get me wrong, I like Bob, but after he mounted me the first time, I thought, "I need my space."

Phyllis: I always felt like a fish out of water. Then while at Harvard Business School I interned as a Mongolian tribeswoman. I found my dream job: yak herding. Now it's just me, my deepest thoughts, and twelve yaks.

Donald: For twenty years I entertained at children's birthday parties before realizing large crowds of kiddies were driving me crazy. Now I stay for only a few minutes, pretend to get an emergency phone call, and leave. The kids and parents hate it but I'm a happy person.

Boyce: It was when I sat down for lunch with some introverted workmates. The table was silent. Aside from one guy who whistled through his nose when he breathed, it sounded like heaven

No Visual Response Home Introvert Test

No Visual Response is the only home introvert test that tells you within minutes if you're an introvert.

How it works

Simply pee on a test strip. Then check the color.

Off-white   Indicates you're an extrovert. Don't tell anyone you took this test. (Since you're an extrovert, you'll probably tell anyway.)

Pink   Indicates you're a mild introvert. You can withstand obnoxious workmates up to eight hours a day as long as you hide in the janitor's closet for occasional breaks.

Green   Indicates you're a normal introvert. You can mingle with a group of strangers at a party until you come up with a good excuse to leave or you find a convenient escape route through an unlocked cellar window.

Blue   Indicates you're a serious introvert. You should only enter into relationships with people who will give you some space, preferably in a neighboring state.

Purple   Indicates you're an extreme introvert. Don't leave your apartment until 2028.

The No Visual Response Home Introvert Test is more accurate than most introvert tests, including the Myers–Briggs Type Indicator (MBTI) assessment, which we recommend if you prefer tests in which you don't have to pee on things.

Web Review:

20,000 Fabulous Things about Introverts

TODD GELLMAN

Being an introvert used to depress me. Then I read an Internet article that changed my life: *20,000 Fabulous Things about Introverts* by Naomi Hamburgman. I learned that my life isn't horrible and depressing; it's great!

I discovered I'm not a lonely guy longing to connect with the rest of the world. I'm a solitary individual who feels more comfortable spending weekends alone, wondering what it's like to have a girlfriend.

I used to hate going to parties at which I didn't know anyone. Naomi has taught me to celebrate my ability to barely get through the evening without wetting my pants.

Spending so much time in my head used to depress me. No more! Yesterday, I thought, "I feel good about myself" 500,000 times!

Before, I couldn't respond quickly to people's questions. But now I've learned to relax and say, "Give me ten minutes and I'll tell you the emergency room phone number."

If you want to celebrate your introversion, go to UnimaginableEcstasy.com and read "20,000 Fabulous Things about Introverts." As Naomi says, "There is a seventy-five percent probability that things couldn't get worse."

Todd Gellman *is a senior data analyst. His desk has been featured in Better Workspaces and Conference Rooms magazine.*

CHAPTER 3

Seeking Solitude: People Who Need People Are the Most Exhausting People in the World

We introverts need, no we *crave* solitude. How much? It varies widely, between twenty-three and one half and twenty-four hours a day.

If you're an introvert like me, you'd rather read this book—or the periodic table—than hang out with thirty "close" friends.

Don't feel bad. It's perfectly normal for introverts. After all, who wants to be at the White House standing in front of a crowd of strangers, accepting your Congressional Medal of Honor, when you could receive a two thumbs up text message?

Contrary to what society or the person begging you to come out of your bedroom says, there's nothing wrong with seeking a life of solitude. It's the most normal thing an introvert can do.

Don't worry if people can't understand why you prefer to sit in silence rather than sing "Sunrise, Sunset" at your cousin's wedding. Plop yourself down on a park bench, put on your best, "I don't want to be disturbed" face, and read on.

Nice Party, Now I'm Ready to Leave

All of us introverts have been there. You go to a party. After a short time, you've had enough socialization and agonizing small talk. You're ready to leave, but your extrovert friend and ride for the evening is having the time of her life. Here are some lines guaranteed to get her out the door pronto.

- I bet your boss would be interested in my multi-level marketing plan.
- I think I'll check out the host's medicine cabinet.
- I know she's a nun but I think she really wants me.
- Tonight's the night I finally open up about my painful rectal itch.
- I've narrowed the guests down to three potential sperm donors.
- This party could use some serious yodeling.

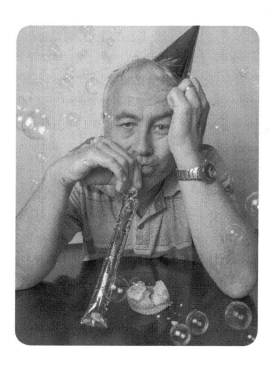

Flee from the Madding Crowd

Donna Dewees is an introvert who has never encountered an uncomfortable social situation she couldn't avoid. "I know how to slip away from any gathering without being noticed. That includes my first, second, and fourth weddings." Dewees, a quiet freelance astrologer trained as a Navy SEAL, uses her survival skills to escape hugging strangers and talkative coworkers. She once fled a noisy bridal shower by squeezing through a tiny bathroom window and rappelling ten stories to a sidewalk, using only a piece of dental floss.

Of course, the best way to avoid any unwanted event is not to go. Donna's first advice: Create an extensive list of excuses. For example, she has twenty-five possible reasons for not attending a Kazakhstani sweet sixteen party. "Although," she says, "my fail-safe excuse is usually, 'I'm under house arrest.'"

If you arrive at your destination but are having second thoughts, Dewees recommends continuing to drive around your end point until you run out of gas. "Then call AAA for help. It's also a good opportunity to listen to your favorite podcasts."

Dewees has advice for introverts who aren't interested in living life off the grid but yearn for more alone time: "Let people know how you feel, but be nice about it. A politely written Post-it note attached to your forehead indicating you're an introvert is always helpful. I guarantee, no one except graphologists and concerned mental health professionals will bother you."

I've Got to Stop Meeting like This

Introverts need a certain amount of alone time—for example, to recover after Cindy in sales punishes you for 120 minutes, rhapsodizing about her vacation plans to Disney World.

There is a point, however, where solitude becomes isolation. Here are some signs you've crossed the line.

- Your inflatable doll says she wants to start seeing other people.
- You recently became a Home Shopping Club Platinum Lifetime Member.
- You're on a first-name basis with each of your toes.
- You ran out of deodorant in 1993.
- You've started replacing words with grunts.
- Even the Jehovah's Witnesses have stopped knocking on your door.
- You're binge-watching Vintage Weather Reports on Netflix.
- Your boyfriend, with whom you've only communicated via Skype, is starting to wonder if you're computer generated.

Ultimate Introvert Vacation Escape:

Chernobyl Deserted Inn

Good news for homebodies who occasionally enjoy exploring the world beyond the hallway to their bathroom: Travel tours for introverts are currently the quiet rage.

Still, introvert travel packages can't shield you totally from exposure to talkative, friendly Midwestern couples telling you where to find the cleanest restroom at the Coliseum.

Are you looking for the total introvert vacation experience? Consider Chernobyl Deserted Inn located off I-95 in Ukraine. Forbes Travel Guide rates it below the Fukushima Motel 6 but slightly above the New Jersey Turnpike Exit 5 rest stop men's room.

Feel everyday worries disappear the second you enter the nuclear contamination zone. The first thing you'll notice is total silence—and the two-headed elk. Don't worry, even the half-men, half-elk won't bother you with needless conversations or invite you to a party.

The Deserted Inn staff couldn't be friendlier, since there isn't any. Choose one of 500 rooms. We recommend one that still has a door and a working lock to keep out the hungry bears—particularly the five-legged hungry bears.

There's plenty to do and see in Chernobyl, including the Plutonium, Safe Energy of Today exhibit (no waiting), Uncle Ivan's Glowing Wax Museum (no waiting), and the birthplace of circus oddity, Sasha, the half-introvert, half-extrovert woman (definitely no waiting).

Make reservations to see Chernobyl now. You only have 20,000 years until it's inhabitable again for humans and extroverts.

Classroom Backseat Basics

For many introverts, home is where the heart is . . . sitting behind the other hearts.

When introverts enter a classroom—or any room—many look for that one special seat in the back. It beckons: "Come, sit, and relax, away from the maddening class."

If you choose to be a sit-in-the-backer, here are some tips to make your rear view stay more enjoyable.

- Sit behind a large person. They're great shields and provide effective soundproofing.

- Always have at least ten excuses handy for when you're caught staring out the window. For example: A) I think I just figured out a cure for cancer. B) That's exactly how the sky looked on the day I was placed in an orphanage.

- Never sit behind a student who enthusiastically participates in class. Watching an arm continually rise for attention can cause severe dizziness.

- If your lifelong dream is to be a ventriloquist, never use students sitting more than ten feet away as practice dummies.

- Some teachers seat their students in alphabetical order, so it wouldn't hurt to change your last name to Zellman.

Funerals Are Great Places to Rendezvous with Your Thoughts

Introvert: Nina Gazoff
Occupation: Part-time CIA agent
Location: I've already said too much

Whenever I need to be alone and clear my head, I go to a funeral. It doesn't have to be for someone I know. In fact, it usually helps if it isn't. Aside from occasional hysterical sobbing, you won't find a more tranquil environment.

There are many memorial services from which to choose. Simply check the obituaries in your local newspaper or online. Ideally, the recently departed should be a complete stranger who died from natural causes. This usually ensures a quiet service with a minimum of drama. You know you've hit pay dirt if you overhear someone say, "It was her time."

I always enter quietly and sit by myself. Mourners rarely talk to me. I have a pretty intense resting bitch face that normally scares the hell out of people. But at funerals, I look like I've lost my best friend which is the effect I'm going for. The only time anyone ever asked why I wasn't smiling was when I attended the funeral of a personal injury attorney.

Aside from the opportunity for contemplation, there's something deeply spiritual about funerals. This age-old ritual of bidding farewell to friends and loved ones always reminds me that I'm part of a vast universe inhabited by introverts, extroverts and grieving widows who are already checking out new prospects on Tinder.

The next time you need to be alone and you're miles from the nearest park, beach or quiet café, go to a funeral. There's no better place to get your required "me" time with a gentle portion of "us" time on the side.

Nina Gazoff *has been employed for thirty-five years by the U.S. government* ■■■■ ■■■ ■■ ■■■■ *and* ■■ *and* ■■ ■■■ ■■ ■■ ■■ ■■ ■■

All Introvert Hangovers Are Not Equal

Introvert hangovers—that exhaustive feeling caused by too much socialization—can be as different as the boisterous extroverts that provoke them. The following are types of hangovers and surefire treatments.

Hangover	Symptom	Remedy
Flapping Tongue Fatigue	Dizziness after being asked for the twentieth time in a job interview, "Why do you want to work here?"	Go to the company's cafeteria or nearest all-you-can eat buffet and rest your head in a plate of potato salad.
No Luckus Interruptus	The beaten and overwhelmed sensation after condo board meetings at which you can never get a word in edgewise	Lie down, relax, and fantasize about a time and place where everyone agrees with you that "We need to replace the lounge chairs around the pool."
Inner Monologue Depletion	Being so tired of people, you can't even talk to the voices in your head.	Concentrate and say to yourself, "Folks, can we continue this conversation another time?" More than anyone, the voices will understand.
Networking Nausea	The woozy feeling that overcomes you after shaking too many regional sales managers' hands.	Hand your business card to the nearest waiter serving shrimp tostada bites, declare victory, and sprint to the warmth and safety of your hotel room.

Loud Afterlife Party Drives Introvert Back from Near-Death Experience

DAISY FELDMAN

I knew something had gone wrong when my emergency liposuction operating surgeon said, "That's it. We did everything we could."

Seconds later, I was hovering over my own body and yelling at him, "No you didn't! You only removed my insurance card!" But nobody heard me.

The next thing I remember is drifting through a quiet tunnel toward a soft glimmering light. I felt I was living in the moment. My never-ending conversation with myself faded away for a few seconds, and I began talking to myself about why my never-ending conversation stopped.

I entered a large, bright room packed shoulder-to-shoulder with people talking and laughing loudly. One by one they approached me and spoke: "How are you? "Any big plans for eternity?" "I still can't get over the great weather we have here." "Why are you so quiet?"

My first impulse was to find a bathroom where I could be alone and gather my thoughts. Then I realized I was now in a place that didn't require bathrooms. I asked myself, is the afterlife just as unaccepting of introverts as the current life? Or maybe it was not my time to die. At this point, it didn't matter; I just wanted to go back.

I slipped out the door and drifted back through the tunnel. The next thing I remember, I was lying on the operating table and a nurse gasped, "Doctor, she's breathing! She's alive!" The doctor responded, "I'll be the judge of that."

Introvert Breaking Points

It's important to know when you've reached your socializing limit. Here are some typical moments that should indicate to an introvert, "no more!"

- When a host says, "Thanks for coming to the party."

- When a boss says, "Moving on to part fifteen, section thirty-two of our role-playing exercise."

- When a stranger at a wedding yells, "Let's do another chicken dance!"

- Immediately after a job interviewer says, "Here's a list of the twelve other people you'll be interviewing with."

- Halfway through your lover asking, "Who's your daddy?"

- When a policeman tells you, "You don't have the right to remain silent."

- When anyone asks, "How was your first day of telemarketing?"

CHAPTER 4

Small Talk: One Tiny Sentence for Man, One Agonizing Moment for Introverts

Why do introverts hate small talk? On one level the answer is simple: We don't like meaningless chatter about the weather, vacations, or the host's clam dip.

But here's what makes it worse: Not only do we find small talk intolerable, we are not very good when we attempt it—basically because we don't have a lot of practice, as opposed to lots and lots of experience avoiding it. We're the ultimate masters of awkward silence.

Think about it. Intellectually superior introverts struggle to say, "How ya doin'?" We can talk to a lifetime PBS contributor about *Downton Abbey*, yet agonize responding to comments like, "Nice tote bag."

So what's an introvert to do? The simple answer is not worry about it. The more realistic answer is learning a few deflective techniques, like saying: "This tote bag is perfect for stuffing unmarked bills during bank heists."

Extrovert's Guide to Making Small Talk with Introverts

We introverts hate small talk. How can you expect us to say hello when we're obsessing about that piece of food stuck in your teeth?

Extroverts need to be more sensitive to the small talk-challenged. Just saying hello to an introvert may cause our eyes to glaze over. Here's a handy Extrovert-to-Introvert Small Talk Conversion chart you can pass on to your extrovert friends.

Instead of saying	Try
Hi.	I bet you're wondering why I'm sporting cleavage down to the wazoo at this funeral.
What do you do for a living?	You look like a doctor friend of mine who went to jail for illegally prescribing OxyContin.
I'm an accountant.	Most people think I'm boring because I'm an accountant, but there are many other reasons I put people to sleep.
Nice party.	This should be interesting. Alice doesn't know her ex-husband and his new girlfriend are coming.
It was nice meeting you.	Wait till I tell my wife I met the guy who broke up her sister's marriage.

Introvert Avoids Small Talk with Omnipotent Attitude

Cassie McCall is a classic introvert. She used to struggle in social situations that required small talk. "Hearing 'Hi, how you doing?' made me nauseated. No one ever asked about my blood sugar levels," she says.

Fortunately, Cassie has found an easy way to avoid small talk. She's mastered a serene facial expression that sends a clear message: I am all-knowing. I have better things to do with my life than talk to you about the weather.

Rather than be offended by her stone-like demeanor, most people are eager to engage her in a deeper conversation. "They think I'm an all-powerful soul who knows every secret of the universe. Heck, I couldn't tell you why they sell underwear in three-packs instead of two."

Cassie has become more socially active since perfecting her omniscient gaze. No longer does she avoid parties and muffler shop openings where she'd normally be forced to talk with people about their plans for vacation. Now I turn my head slowly, look out a window, and shed a single tear. In no time we're chatting about the futility of life."

Cassie McCall believes all introverts have the ability to avoid small talk. "Most extroverts are freaked out by our quietness. Don't worry if someone asks 'How they hanging?' You can say anything as long as you say it with an empty stare.

Sextroverting Can Be a Multisyllabic Turn-On

Just because introverts are small-talk averse doesn't mean we can't enjoy a little sensual messaging. Keep your key-play intense and complex. Use the following chart to take your complex touch taps to smoldering heights.

Popular sexting phrase	Sextroverting alternative
What are you wearing?	I respond very well to visual stimuli, particularly when it comes to women's couture. I'd be curious to know if you are sporting anything intended to arouse the male species.
I think your lips are really sensuous.	Not to detract from other parts of your anatomy, but I'd venture to say your lips, especially the bottom one, are your strongest feature.
I want to take you to a place called orgasmland	Are you familiar with a township known as Orgasmland? I'm quite certain you won't find it on Google Maps.
Your bulge is driving me mad.	It's really a strange phenomenon that even I have a hard time processing, but I'm quite overwhelmed by your growing expression of affection for me.
I'd love to ride you.	I have to confess, we may be moving toward interspecies fantasies.

Man Survives Titanic Sinking While Avoiding Bringing Attention to Himself

Most people are familiar with the British passenger liner *Titanic*. On April 15, 1912 during its maiden voyage, it struck an iceberg and sank to the bottom of the North Atlantic Ocean taking with it more than 1,500 passengers.

Few people are familiar with one of the 498 survivors, introvert Felix Flambeau, an itinerant toothpick designer from Boonton, New Jersey, who was taking his first-ever vacation. Initially, he was having the time of his life: avoiding passengers, avoiding the crowded buffet lines, and avoiding invitations to enter limbo contests.

All that changed on the evening of April 15 when, while seeking some solitude underneath an unoccupied deck chair, he spotted an enormous iceberg ahead of the ship.

Sensing the seriousness of the situation but not wanting to engage a crewmember in conversation, Flambeau leaped into action. He made a mental note to write a warning note and slip it under the captain's door the next morning.

Tragically, the *Titanic* struck the iceberg and began to sink. Rather than join fellow passengers in a crowded, noisy lifeboat, Flambeau dived off the ship's bow and floated alone in the ice-cold water for two days. During this time, rescue ships passed within whispering distance, but he remained silent, not wanting to attract attention to himself. Finally, he was rescued by an Argentine trawler which had spotted "a strange man floating in the water writing postcards." For the solitary gentleman from Boonton, New Jersey, it was the most peaceful and enjoyable part of his vacation.

Toastmasters Introduces Introvert Small Talk Workshops

Toastmasters, the organization dedicated to helping people become better public speakers, is adding new workshops for introverts who want to improve their small talk skills. Topics include:

- First impressions: Transforming a severely sarcastic sigh into a barely detectable groan.

- Saying "Hi" without crib notes.

- Staring at a woman's breasts is not "almost" making eye contact.

- When is it not appropriate to query, "Is this handsome guy your boyfriend or a paid escort?"

- Listening without snoring.

- How to clean up limericks using suitable words that rhyme with "Nantucket."

- Ten nice things to say to a person handcuffed to an FBI agent.

- Five resting bitch faces guaranteed to project empathy.

- Visual aids and props: Things that are better left said by your hand puppet.

- Catchy comebacks after forty-five minutes of awkward silence.

CHAPTER 5

Stuck Inside Your Head: I Had Me at Hello

Why are so many introverts consumed by their own thoughts? Is it because of the way our brains are wired? Maybe, but there has to be another reason. Dammit! I just missed my exit. Now, I'm going to be late. Remember to take the next exit. Where was I? Oh yeah, buried in my thoughts. Are we too inwardly focused? If so, is it because we're introverts? Maybe we're just super-enlightened. What's so enlightened about thinking about the same things over and over? Darn it! I missed the next exit again! Come on, focus! Get out of your head! Repeat after me, I'm not going to miss the next exit. I'm not going miss the next exit. I'm not going to—oops, missed it again.

How Did You Meet Your Inner Voice?

Patty: We met at a high school dance. Everyone ignored me. I felt lonely and depressed until I heard myself say, "Patty, the heck with them, let's go home and read Anne of Green Gables. We've been inseparable ever since.

Bob: In kindergarten, Donna Wheelwright told everyone I wet my blanket during naptime. I screamed to myself, "That's not true, you made that up!" continually for the next twenty-two years. It's nice to know I can talk to me about anything.

Neil: Another voice in my head fixed us up. At first I thought I was full of myself, and vain. Now I see it was my way of hiding my insecurities. I've really grown to love me.

Hillary: I was staring out the window during a philosophy class at Wellesley College. The wind blew a wave of leaves across the quad, and I said to myself, "Marry a brilliant scoundrel and then eventually run for president."

Get Away from It All,
Be at One in the Mall

Introverts need sacred places of solitude to ponder and decompress. Nowhere will you find a more peaceful environment for your contemplation-palooza than a desolate shopping mall.

Let your mind wander while strolling down long corridors past the remaining open stores. Gaze at colorful "For Rent" signs and feel your blood pressure drop. Observe the remaining kiosk while glancing away from its intrepid owner.

Today, Old Navy is manned by one guy who still can't believe he has an MBA and is managing an Old Navy store. His hard luck is your opportunity. Finally, no chirpy sales clerk to ask, "Can I help you?" while you're thinking about words that rhyme with "archaic."

If you really need some serious alone time, head over to Sears—if it doesn't close its doors permanently before you arrive. Asking for directions to the hardware department is almost a near-death experience.

For the more spiritually inclined, there's no better place to meditate than at Cinnabon. Have the pick of every seat. No extra charge for the sugar rush.

Eventually, shopping malls will go the way of chatrooms and Leonard Cohen fan clubs. Introverts will move on to their next fortress of solitude. Until then, a fading Footlocker franchise beckons: "Come, sit, we'll ignore you."

Top Ten Inner Voice Conversation Starters

1. Nice brain. Who's my decorator?

2. Am I seeing any other voices?

3. How was my day?

4. Do I talk to myself in the nude?

5. I look good. Have I been working out?

6. Do I sing to myself in the shower?

7. Where am I from?

8. Who do I think is the luckiest person in this head?

9. Hi, do I work here?

10. So what do I do for a living?

Man Walks Across U.S. While Obsessing about Next Summer's Vacation

Don Macomber, a plumber from Philadelphia, walked 3,876 miles across the United States to raise money and awareness for blistered foot sufferers. He hiked the entire distance while obsessing about his vacation plans for next summer.

Don kept a journal, chronicling the parts of the trip he could remember, starting with a close call in Indiana while walking absentmindedly in the middle of a busy highway. "I was thinking about renting a cottage next July and August on the Jersey Shore, and the next thing I know I'm in the passing lane."

He doesn't remember a thing about crossing Iowa or Nebraska. "Cornfields come to mind, and I recall asking myself, 'Should buy SPF 15 or 30 sunscreen when I go to the beach?'"

Macomber assumes he met countless people during his long trek. "I vaguely remember a very nice woman offering me a glass of water in Illinois or Colorado. These acts of kindness from strangers, most of which I don't recall, reaffirm my love of mankind."

This was to be Don's only long-distance walk, "although I may have hiked the Appalachian Trail last month. I seem to remember something about wrestling a black bear in my pup tent."

CHAPTER 6

Why Are You So Quiet? A Babbling World Wants to Know

The question that we introverts are asked most frequently is "Why are you so quiet?" The second most asked question is "Why does it bother you every time I ask, "Why are you so quiet?"

Despite every possible thoughtful explanation, the extrovert's response is usually the same:

- Why is she so upset? I only ask her that question once a day.

- She's never liked me. I could talk about outlet store shopping until I'm blue in the face, and she sits there saying nothing.

- All he cares about is himself. Why didn't he ask about my visit to the proctologist?

In the end, it really doesn't matter what people think about our quiet nature, because this is America (if you're reading this book in the U.S.). You have the right to remain silent.

If an Introvert is Silent in a Forest, Does it Still Annoy Extroverts?

When they go noisy, we go passive aggressive

Nothing drives extroverts crazier than an introvert's tendency to be quiet Scientists are unsure why they require a constant stream of verbal stimulation. After all, who wouldn't want to sit alone contemplating life for days at a time? However, until a cure is found, we introverts must endure an endless stream of queries about our lack of verbal communication.

Here are some helpful responses to popular inquiries.

When they say	You say
Why are you so quiet?	Actually, I'm speaking to my dog but at a frequency only he can understand.
You haven't said a word all evening.	Excuse me, I've been talking nonstop to myself since the waiter seated us.
Talking to you is like talking to the wall.	At least with the wall I have a fighting chance to get a word in edgewise.
Am I boring you?	No, I'm absolutely fascinated by the way your left eye slowly drifts to the left.
You didn't say a thing to my friends.	Doesn't vigorously staring count for anything?
Your silence scares me.	And to think I was going to surprise you next week by thinking "Happy Birthday."

Finding Someone Who Is Soothed by Your Sounds of Silence

When looking for a mate, it's not easy to find that special person who will understand your quietness, but some people are uniquely qualified to deal with soft spoken souls.

British Queen's Guard: These guys are paid to spend each day in total silence. A few more minutes with you should be a piece of cake.

Librarian: No one treasures your silence more than a librarian. Aside from an occasional spirited discussion about the Dewey Decimal System, they love their shush-free moments.

Mime: Three unspoken words: He gets you.

Shepherd: Aside from an occasionally concerned sheep and a gossipy Border Collie, no one listens to his problems. He won't expect you to be any different.

Captors Forced to Endure Silent Treatment from Introverted Prisoners

A much-anticipated congressional report investigating torture methods carried out by the government's security agency revealed the extent to which introverted captives inflict emotional damage on their interrogators.

"They seem to thrive on isolation and silence" said one agent. "Even when we try to be friendly, they don't talk. Frankly, it hurts our feelings."

Report after report describes the introverted prisoners as "silent," "arrogant," "standoffish," and "stuck up." An interrogator recounts, "I got so frustrated, I screamed 'Why are you so quiet?' He just looked at me and said, 'Why can't you stop yapping? Waterboarding is more stimulating than your dimwitted tête-à-tête.'"

The prisoners' behavior mystified the most seasoned agents. "Why don't they want to talk about the weather or the Kardashians?" was a frequently asked question. "The only time the introverted prisoners get visibly upset is when we remove them from solitary confinement."

The captors' frustration was summed up by one agent: "I put down my whip and electric cattle prod in exasperation and screamed, 'Why aren't you saying anything?' The prisoner responded, 'It's not as if I'm not thinking anything.'"

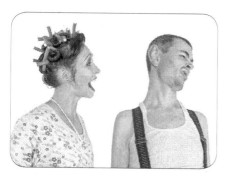

Wrong Things to Say When an Extrovert Asks "Are You Okay?"

It drives introverts crazy. We're minding their own business in silence with a dreary expression on our face, as introverts sometimes do, and someone asks, "Are you okay?"

Unfortunately, "yes" is never a good enough answer. Nor are the following.

- Okay? I haven't felt this great since you asked me if I was okay two minutes ago.

- Thanks for your concern, but I'm just giving my facial muscles a rest.

- Could you repeat your question? I was communicating with my therapist, Satan.

- I'd like to smile, but I become dizzy every time I turn my frown upside down.

- I'll be okay once the drugs wear off—or kick in. I forget which one.

Incredible Hulk Erupts after Date Asks "Why Are You So Quiet?"

Chaos ensued at a local eatery after mild-mannered Bruce Banner's blind date continued to ask him, "Why are you so quiet?" Banner could finally take it no longer and involuntarily transformed into the raging Incredible Hulk. The owner of Le Petit Horreur Café is still totaling the damages.

Sheryl Panzoni, who met Banner through the dating website Mating-MadScientists.com, had no idea he had an alter ego. "He said he possessed superhuman strength, but everybody embellishes their personal ads. Bruce had a cute smile, so I agreed to meet him for dinner."

She said her date with Banner began uneventfully. "But after a while I was getting tired of carrying the conversation. I asked if there was something wrong and he said no." Panzoni continued questioning him about his quiet nature until she noticed a slight change in his demeanor. "His body started to grow, he turned green, and he started to grunt. I thought, 'Oops!' At this point I knew he was not going to drive me home."

Within seconds, Bruce Banner had transformed into the Incredible Hulk and began destroying the eatery. As customers fled, Panzoni pleaded with Banner/Hulk, "You don't have to talk. We can just sit and eat!" The Hulk ignored her and continued demolishing the hostess station.

Despite the evening ending with her date being dragged away by twenty National Guardsmen, Sheryl Panzoni has no regrets. "Months later he sent me a lovely note apologizing for his behavior. The evening didn't go well, but I came to admire his quiet dignity—and he was still nicer than most guys I meet online."

Awaken the Strong and Inaudible You

The Learning Annex is proud to present Luther Spivak, entrepreneur, pushup champion, silent auctioneer, and author of the best-selling pamphlet, "All Quiet on the Western Front of My Mouth."

Luther will present a short history of strong and silent types: from Orga, the first cavewoman to wrestle and then briefly date a wild hyena, to Gary Cooper, an actor so quiet he didn't realize movies had sound until his fifteenth talkie.

Luther will next quietly, yet assertively, talk about his five easy steps to becoming a more confident and less audible you.

1. Rid a town overrun with evildoers without saying more than three words. Then quietly get on your horse and ride away.

2. Ask a needy, hysterical, overly emotional person out for a date. Calmly and silently listen to their problems. Then quietly excuse yourself, pretend to go to the bathroom, and never return.

3. Join a local branch of Toastmasters. When it's your turn to speak, stand up, say "yup," and then quietly head for the nearest exit.

4. Attend your high school reunion. After the tenth classmate asks, "Are you still quiet?" softly reply "Are still angry you were wait-listed at our local community college?" Then drive away in the Rolls-Royce you rented to impress everyone.

5. At a ceremony for winning the Nobel Peace Prize, announce to the audience you've mistakenly left your acceptance speech in your other tuxedo/purse. Then take out your cell phone and walk away, while having an important pretend conversation with the president of Brazil.

CHAPTER 7

Trying to Be Heard in a Herd

It's easy to express yourself when sitting alone watching a beautiful sunset. Adding people to the mix makes things more difficult for introverts—especially after someone begins to drone on about the gorgeous sunset they witnessed during a court-imposed trash pickup detail alongside Route 85 in 1987.

How can we introverts be heard? The simple answer is to jump into the conversation—if only it were that easy for us to jump into any discussion. Unfortunately for us, thoughtful listening has never been an effective tool for getting people's attention.

Until the world learns to respect our awesome silence, we must rely on more subtle ways to be heard, like faking a heart attack or banging Morse code on the table with our foreheads.

Finally, Protection from Seamless Conversations!

Do you enjoy talking to more than one person at a time, but can never get a word in edgewise?

Do you wish people would stop talking for JUST TWO FREAKIN' SECONDS so you can be heard?

ZIP IT – *Extra Strength for Introverts*® silences nonstop talking. Simply spray **ZIP IT** at the offending yakker. Then say what's on your mind.

ZIP IT *stops:*

- ✔ People who love the sound of their voice
- ✔ Committee chairpersons who aren't interested in what others have to say
- ✔ Amateur orators who never get to the point
- ✔ Know-it-alls who could not care less about your opinion
- ✔ Repeat offenders who say the same thing over and over and over
- ✔ Deep breathers who can speak for hours without coming up for air
- ✔ Persons petrified of pregnant pauses

ZIP IT comes in two strengths: *Clam Up* and *Put a Cork in It* for family get-togethers.

Advice from Andy Brightman:
Rendered Speechless

Dear Andy: I'm a board member for a nonprofit organization. We're raising money to restore the nation's first solar-powered rendering facility. Our monthly meetings are lively affairs in which opinions fly fast and furious. I have much to say, but there's never a pause in the conversation for me to speak. I'm an extreme introvert and could never interrupt someone, but I need to express how I feel about converting waste animal tissue. How can I share my thoughts with the group?

Bursting on Beacon Hill

Dear Bursting: I too have a hard time making myself heard in meetings. It's not easy for introverts to cut people off and join the verbal fray. We have to devise alternative strategies that work best for us. For example, I always bring my ventriloquist dummy, Tommy to meetings. He isn't afraid to jump into any conversation. However, there's no guarantee your dummy will be as extroverted as Tommy.

You have a right to be heard. The world needs to know how you feel about dead animal carcasses. The key is finding a way to communicate that works for you that won't result in lawsuits or restraining orders.

Andy Brightman *is a former CIA intelligence officer.* To Hell and Back: My Thirty-Five Years in Cubicle 289D *is his recently published autobiography.*

Interrupting a Blathering Express

Trying to get a word in edgewise with extroverts is like driving onto a busy freeway; you'll never make it if you strictly obey the yield sign.

Here are some simple things you can say that can make the difference between getting your two cents in and going home with change in your pocket.

To politely interrupt someone, try saying:

- Just an observation: When you started talking, I didn't have a beard.

- This is the first time I've seen someone's clothes go out of style as they spoke.

- I need to speak now. My doctor says I only have seventy years to live.

When someone tries to interrupt you, try saying:

- I was polite enough to listen to your position, which I believe you began explaining during the Clinton administration.

- Go ahead. I normally finish my thoughts in mid-sentence.

- You'll have plenty of time to speak after I finish my eulogy.

CHAPTER 8

Take This Job and Tolerate It: An Introvert's Guide to Gainful Employment

They never tell us introverts on Career Day in high school that you can't manage a multinational corporation from the privacy of your bedroom. That's key information. The workplace is a challenging environment for us. Unfortunately, it was designed for guys named Cal who orgasm when they're named "employee of the week."

Until recently, work settings have catered to extroverts. There are very few job descriptions that read "Looking for a person who excels at living, breathing, and eating each day with a bunch of self-promoting livewires. Must have a bone-crushing handshake." It's just assumed.

Fortunately, society is beginning to learn the value of introverts in the workplace. The bad news is your company may be throwing a giant "meet the introverts" mixer.

The solution for introverts is simple: You need a job, any job, so you carve out a little piece of passive-aggressive paradise in a cubicle or, God forbid, open space layout wasteland. Signing daily birthday cards for face-less fellow workmates is a small price to pay for health insurance with sky-high deductibles and a nearly worthless 401k.

The workplace may someday be more welcoming toward introverts. In the meantime, relax, take your regular seat in the back of the conference room, put on your best resting bitch face, and imagine this is your dream job: pan flutist in an enchanted forest.

Bottom Seven Job Interview Tips for Introverts

1. Find out who's interviewing you and learn everything you can about them. But don't let them see you parked outside their house with binoculars.

2. Prepare. Write down questions you may be asked. Rehearse the answers like: "No, I'm not catatonic." Or, "My biggest strength is my ability to answer questions I've barely heard because I was buried in my own thoughts."

3. Go to as many job interviews as you can if only to practice your interview skills. Don't stop until you can make it through one interview without perspiration stains ruining your best suit.

4. Emphasize your strengths as an introvert. For example, "If you need someone to quietly stand in the ladies' room and make sure everyone is washing their hands, I'm your woman."

5. Only apply for introvert-friendly jobs. You'd be surprised how many intelligent, solitary souls answer want ads for "Cock Fight Crowd Coordinator."

6. If making eye contact is too hard, connect with your interviewer using jazz hands.

7. When asked to list your accomplishments, avoid answers like: "Making it this far in the interview without throwing up."

Walmart Hires Its First Introverted Greeter

Walmart has hired its first self-described introvert as a greeter. Walter Ronko, a seventy-six-year-old retired file clerk, began work recently at a store in Tranquilo, Arizona.

Ronko, who hasn't smiled voluntarily since 1963, said he has always avoided occupations that require social interaction. "When I saw the want ad for Walmart greeter, I thought, 'Why would I want a job where I have to be friendly to strangers all day?' Then I remembered something that happened years ago. I briefly dated a dominatrix named Janice.

"Our relationship didn't last long. We attended different churches and had dissimilar tastes in spiked collars. But I fondly recall our candlelit dinners, walks on the beach, and being handcuffed to a radiator while being ordered to bark like a dog. Deep down, I still feel like I've been a very bad boy and I need to be punished. That's why I'm working at Walmart."

Torture is one thing, but an extremely introverted person cheerfully subjecting himself to babbling strangers eight hours a day is beyond agony. "Welcoming folks with a smile is particularly tough," he says. "Lately I've started wearing a set of grinning wax lips. It scares the hell out of some kids, but so do most Walmart shoppers."

Surviving Team-Building Exercises

Nothing elevates an introvert's blood pressure more than a good team-building exercise. It's like a Bataan Death March with fewer bathroom breaks.

Look on the bright side. Your colleagues know you as that sullen woman who never talks to anyone and hasn't looked up from her laptop in meetings since 2008. What better way to show your office mates there's more to you than the back of your head?

Here are some team-building survival tips. They can make the difference between a horrifying experience and a merely traumatic episode easily managed with generous doses of psychotropic drugs.

- Team-building exercises frequently begin with each participant telling everyone something interesting about themselves. This is a trap. Do you really want HR to know you enjoy collecting stamps in the nude?

- Before the trust game, offer to clean the room of hidden listening devices.

- Every time the spotlight of attention is pointed at you, mumble something about "a traitor in our midst."

- In every problem-solving situation, say: "I know a guy who can make that go away for $500, no questions asked."

- When all else fails, revert to the fetal position.

Dealing with Networking Difficulties

Networking for introverts is like listening thoughtfully for extroverts. It can be torture with a touch of agony. Meeting new people is a big part of that process, even if means meeting marketing mavens named Hal from San Mateo.

Here are some easy-to-learn techniques that can help you survive overly aggressive handshakes from sales reps and mind-numbing small talk with anyone named Jennifer in technical support.

Set realistic goals. For your first networking event, write down your objectives, then congratulate yourself. For your second networking event, plan to actually attend. You're really making progress now!

Always smile. This is not easy if your normal facial expression resembles someone being strapped into an electric chair. It may take time to retrain your facial muscles. In the meantime, simply insert a Popsicle stick horizontally in your mouth and bite down. You'll look insanely happy and land your next big account in no time.

Ask a lot of questions. Your questions don't have to be about anything relevant to the occasion. For example: How many paid pagan holidays does your company have?

Talk to someone who is alone. He or she will welcome anyone who will listen to their endless diatribe about negative market trends in Peoria. And if it's another introvert, you can both recharge by staring at each other's shoes in awkward silence.

Follow up. If the conversation becomes uncomfortable, claim to be your identical twin sister who has some jealously issues. Then apologize and promise to get some professional help.

Take Me to Your Quiet Leader

Do you think being an introvert prevents you from being a successful leader? Think again. Just because large groups of people aren't your cup of tea doesn't mean you can't boss them around.

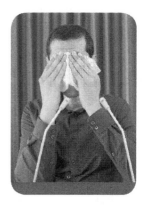

Follow these simple business management rules. In no time, employees whom you can barely greet with a guttural "good morning" will swoon after one of your barely audible "g'nights."

Be yourself: Unless you can impersonate other famous successful introverts like Bill Gates, Eleanor Roosevelt or President Rutherford B. Hayes.

Inspire others: Your employees may think you're aloof and standoffish. They'll forget quickly after you tell them you saw Jesus in a toner cartridge.

Project an air of quiet confidence: If possible, without whistling nervously through your nose.

Delegate more: If the janitor is a whiz at cleaning toilets, there's no reason he can't take your place at an Amazon board of directors meeting.

Avoid people burnout: Interacting with countless folks all day is exhausting for introverts. Teach a pet parrot on your shoulder to say, "Let's run it up the flag pole and then take it offline."

Schmooze It or Lose It

Asking an introvert to master the fine art of schmoozing is like asking an extrovert to gather his thoughts; it ain't gonna happen.

But fear not. You don't have to be a super schmoozer to advance your career—especially if your career is counting crullers and Dunkin' Donuts. Just follow these simple steps.

- Appear to be a good listener. Nod your head every few seconds. If you become sleepy, count the speaker's freckles.

- Pretend to be open and genuine. Then pretend to faint when it's obvious you're not fooling anyone.

- People expect a firm handshake to be followed with eye contact and small talk. Take a different approach. Squeeze the hand until you feel a bone break. Then spend the rest of the evening searching your phone for the closest emergency room.

- Master the art of pretend conversation. Always respond with "I hear you," "You don't have to tell me," or "You're the boss." Or simply combine them with, "I hear you don't have to tell me you're the boss."

- Be prepared for when you forget a person's name. For example, you may not remember the name of your marketing VP because you're totally focused on his bad breath. Just make sure you don't address him as "Mr. Garlic and Onions."

Unleashing Your Inner Willy Loman

It's time to let the world know what you have to offer—even if you're offering two-for-one deals on recycled tube socks.

We get it. You're an introvert. You don't like bringing attention to yourself. But it's hard to succeed if no one knows you or what you do unless you're being monitored by Homeland Security.

Using just a few of your introvert strengths, you can show the world what you have to offer.

Listen and observe: For example, after one short conversation, you may conclude: "This is the perfect person with whom to merge my multinational corporation" or "Why doesn't he trim his ear hairs?"

Prepare what to say: Memorize your talking points. If that's too hard, bring along a portable teleprompter.

Share your experiences: People may not connect your face with your business card, but they'll never forget the woman who talked about being abducted by a UFO.

Build meaningful connections: Don't focus on meeting lots of people. Rather, build a relationship with the assistant data entry clerk with whom you chatted for hours about migratory robots.

Be honest with yourself: When in doubt, look in the mirror and give it to yourself straight. After all, no one knows you better than you—and perhaps your therapist who plans make you the subject of her next book.

There Is an I in "I Don't Want to Be on a Team"

We've all been there. You are asked at a job interview: *Do you enjoy working with a team?*

Inside your head, you're screaming "Hell no!" Another voice surrenders: "I need to pay my rent and feed my iguana." So you gather your strength and respond, "I was born to work on a team."

Wouldn't it be great if you could answer that question honestly and still get the job? Here are some "finesse" responses.

- What's not to love about discussing cubicle etiquette during five-hour department meetings?

- Does teeming with anger count?

- I believe in teams. In fact, a team of wild horses dragged me to his job interview.

- I'm a team player, but I only high-five coworkers after they apply hand sanitizer.

- There's no better team player than I—as my long-time workmate and pet turtle can attest.

Introvert Porn Star Seeks Solitude in Swinging Setting

BY SHY SKYLER

Dear Diary,

Today I begin my new job as a porn star. I hope being an introvert won't prevent me from succeeding as it did when I was a court jester at a Saudi Arabian Renaissance Faire.

8:00 a.m. I hang out by the donuts and condoms, hoping no one will notice me. Betty, the company accountant, introduces herself, and we have an interesting conversation about tax shelters and multiple orgasms caused by excessive trampoline play.

9:15 a.m. My co-star, Tiffany Spiegelman is immediately in my face with insipid questions like, "How long is your penis?" and "Would you like to have a threesome with the UPS guy?" Just once I'd like to meet someone who enjoys talking about more meaningful things like Zen and the art of anonymous restroom sex.

9:45 a.m. The director keeps telling me to grunt and groan more. Small and insignificant moaning has never been easy for me, so I start panting T.S. Eliot's "The Waste Land." After eight minutes, they assume I'm having a seizure and call 911.

1:45 p.m. While servicing a naughty nurse and a transgender pizza delivery person, an albino dominatrix keeps asking, "Why are you so quiet?" Finally, I scream, "Because I'm an introverted cabana boy, dammit!" I thought I ruined the scene, but the director yells "That's great! Use it!"

2:30 p.m. The orgy starts and I'm body surfing over two sets of chubby twins. After coming up for air the third time I'm ready to go home.

4:45 p.m. Back at my apartment at last! I fall into my large, comfortable reading chair, and decompress. Nicole, my cat strolls across the room without showing the slightest inclination she wants to be stroked. She really gets me.

I Want to Be Alone—
But I Need This Job

Did you hear the great news? Employers now love introverts! For example, some organizations have instituted daily thirty-minute fist bump moratoriums.

If your company hasn't reached this level of enlightenment, you may need to creatively seek out new and innovative quiet spaces. Here are some examples.

- Sitting alone in the company cafeteria while wondering why you gave up on your dream of being a jazz bassoonist can be emotionally restorative—until coworkers stop by to say hello or ask about the Gambino account. Stop them in their tracks by saying, "I want to talk to you about Scientology" and then return to your self-absorption.

- Restrooms are great places for quality alone time. Tape an "Out of Order" sign to an empty stall, and you've created your private reading room.

- Fill your cubicle with bottles of pills while wearing a surgical mask. Continually reassure your coworkers, "My doctor says it's *probably* not contagious." Then sit back and listen to the silent sounds of an empty office wing.

- Following an emotionally exhausting three-hour status meeting, consider fleeing to the tranquil setting of your parked car's trunk. No one understands your need for solitude more than your spare tire.

CHAPTER 9

Finding Love and Intimacy from a Comfortable Distance

When it comes to close personal relationships, the challenge for introverts is clear: "I love you. I want to spend eternity with you. Now if you'll excuse me, I need to be alone."

As potential partners, we introverts have a lot to offer. For example, we're good listeners. In fact, we comprise twenty-nine of the last thirty Court Stenographer Hall of Fame inductees.

Introverts are great conversationalists. Aside from avoiding small talk and those long periods of time when we're silent, we are virtually one-person Algonquin Round Tables.

And of course, we are great lovers, at least according to introverts who blog on the Internet that introverts are great lovers.

Alas, finding a suitable lover is not easy for people who spend seventy-five percent of their time thinking about finding a suitable lover. Don't despair. It's just a matter of time before that certain someone, who recognizes the special person that you are, enters your life and seductively whispers, "Has anyone ever said you have an adorable resting bitch face?"

Dating World, Here I Come!

You've been pretty productive lately. You finally found a gym that doesn't prosecute members for failing to wipe down the machines. And after a lifetime of wondering if you suffer from Square Peg in Round Hole syndrome, you discovered you're simply an introvert.

Now it's time to find someone with whom to share your wonderful, solitary life.

Before posting an online a photo of your trembling face feigning confidence, take a deep breath, relax, and read the following tips.

Don't panic. It may take some time, but eventually nervousness will be the last thing you'll be thinking about as you head out to meet your fifty-ninth "sure thing."

Think about the kind of person you'd like to meet. Should he be tall and brooding? If so, must he be able to dunk a basketball? Should she have a pleasant blank stare? If so, is a complete set of teeth mandatory?

Don't worry about rejection. Unlike most extroverts who, after a bad date, must go home to a lonely, empty apartment, you get to go home to a *great,* empty apartment.

Be yourself. You are a wonderful person with much to offer, including the ability to quietly listen to your date talk endlessly without changing your facial expression or losing consciousness (most of the time).

Be up-front about your introversion. Better to get these things out in the open so your date doesn't interrupt the evening by calling 911 to report an unresponsive body.

Be patient. It takes even the most seasoned daters at least ten encounters to comfortably say, "You don't look anything like the photo in your personal ad."

Passion des Introvertis

He: I love that you respect my space. Let's meet in the living room on Thursday.

She: It's wonderful we don't clutter our lives with meaningless small talk. I just wish there was a way I could tell you we're out of toilet paper.

He: Did I tell you how much I cherish you, that my life began when we first met, and my existence is meaningless without you? Or was I just thinking that?

She: I treasure that I don't have to explain my peaceful silent nature to you, and why it's so exhausting for me to say, "I treasure that I don't have to explain my peaceful silent nature to you."

He: It's wonderful we never have house guests. It means more onion dip for us.

She: I feel closest to you when you respect my need to be alone, especially when I'm wearing headphones during sex.

He: You're the first person who's never asked me, "What are you thinking?"—when I was having a seizure.

She: I respect your privacy and will never ask why I've never met your family. Your alien pod story is good enough for me.

Couple Celebrates Fifty Years of Barely Talking

When John Fenamore and David Clamup sat next to each other at a home insecticide disposal lecture fifty years ago, they had no idea it was the beginning of a quiet relationship that would culminate in marriage forty-nine years later.

"I didn't notice him at first," said Fenamore, the retired CEO of Quickie Muffler. "Then Dave accidentally spilled a container of DDT on me. I said, 'Hey,' and he said 'Sorry.'"

Clamup, a semi-retired metal detector repair technician, remembers that moment as if it were yesterday. "That's right. I said, "'Sorry.'"

The two quiet men immediately sensed a chemistry between them and started seeing each other on a regular basis. For the next three years their conversations consisted of "Yup," "Nope," "Fine with me," and "Why not?"

The couple's close and loving relationship is quickly apparent. They never look at each other and easily complete each other's moments of silence. Asked if they could describe their husband's eyes, both men said, "two."

Fenamore and Clamup moved in together in 1967. John remembers fondly, "We didn't say a word to each other until 1973. Good times."

The silent partners finally married last year. Their wedding announcement read simply, "We said 'I do' and we did."

Top Ten Introvert Sexting Lines

1. You're so hot. I want you in another state.

2. I don't mean to brag but I can go as long as I can obsess.

3. Give me some small talk and make it hurt.

4. The other voice in my head likes to watch.

5. You're like my annoying boss. I can't stop thinking about you.

6. I get so horny when you don't say anything.

7. You wear me out like a twenty-five minute organizational meeting.

8. I'm going to drive you beyond ecstasy and then give you some alone time.

9. You're so sexy when you don't look at me.

10. I'd love to watch you decompress in the nude.

Introvert Couple of the Week
Artist's models never hide anything from each other

Sheila and Hank are nude artist's models and introverts. In addition to being passionate about standing quietly unclothed for hours, they also share a love for deep conversation and perfectly sculptured love handles.

Hank: We met on the dating website, EmbarrassingRashMates.com. Our first date was at a small, intimate café. We spent the whole evening talking about allergic eczema.

Sheila: We quickly realized we had so much in common: an appreciation for solitude, quiet thoughtful conversation, and an aversion to cold metal seats.

Hank: I feel blessed Sheila has chosen me to not share her most trivial thoughts with.

Sheila: We can be happy simply lying in each other's arms, not talking about the weather. In fact, sometimes we don't talk until four in the morning.

Hank: Sheila has made me a better artist's model. Before I met her, I would sometimes stand for hours, obsessing about a horsefly walking across my buttock. Now I dream about the two of us, standing lovingly hand-in-hand, trying not to be noticed by an IKEA salesperson.

Sheila: Hank knows me better than anyone. I may earn a living posing naked in front of art students, but I've never exposed my heart to anyone but him—and the surgical team that performed my triple bypass.

CHAPTER 10

Introvert/Extrovert Relationships: You Say Potato, I Say Enough Small Talk

Introverts/extrovert relationships can be challenging but often provide a good counterbalance—at least in relationships that don't end up on the six o'clock news: "Complete living room set tossed from third-story apartment. More at eleven."

Frequently, introverts need extroverts to coax them out of their shells, or in extreme cases, out of a burning house. Whereas extroverts often need introverts to remind them to take their Ritalin and write thank-you notes to their 5,000 close friends.

There are trade-offs in all relationships. Yes, it's nice to be with a like-minded, introverted soul who "gets you." However, vibrations caused by your intense discussions can cause dishes to fall off shelves.

And you may not like being dragged to parties by your more outgoing mate, but who knows, you may meet an occasional introvert hiding in the bathroom, bedroom, or next to the clam dip.

You Get Me, You Kind of Get Me

Relationships are never easy, but relationships between introverts and extroverts pose unique challenges.

Just ask Susanne, an introvert and Jeremy, an extrovert.

Jeremy: Growing up, my family frowned upon introverts. My father used to say, "I have no respect for a man who won't bring attention to himself in large gatherings of strangers."

Susanne: My family felt the same way about extroverts. My uncle was shunned after he asked a stranger for directions.

Jeremy: Susanne and I met at a party. I was chest-bumping fifteen or twenty of my closest friends. She was sitting alone reading the instructional manual for the host's DVR.

Susanne: I was halfway through the troubleshooting section when I sensed someone was watching me. I looked up and it was Jeremy.

Jeremy: I didn't realize she was an introvert. I thought she was a hot babe who worked for the cable company.

Susanne: It's corny but true; when you meet the right person, love—and separate apartments—will keep you together.

Introvert's Life Opens Up with Help of Extrovert Therapy Dog

Pamela (not her real name), a freelance 100 proofreader for a vodka trade magazine, is an extreme introvert who needs and values her time alone. But she also wants to experience things that her solitary lifestyle prevents, like meeting exiled foreign dictators and contra dancing.

She attempted to find a suitable date on websites like SexyShutIns.com and eHarmosexuals.org with no success. She eventually heard about an organization that matches introverts with extrovert therapy dogs (ETD).

"My life changed immediately for the better," said Pamela. "On our first walk, Tad (not his real name), my ETD, introduced me, well, pulled me to a woman hailing a cab, a man fixing a tire, and a couple arguing about money. If I was by myself I wouldn't have noticed them."

Like a lot of introverts, Pamela values being alone but also desires exposure to the outside world extroverts can provide. "For many introverts like me, an extrovert is my window to parts unknown. Before I met Tad I had no idea packs of feral dogs congregated behind dumpsters in back allies."

Pamela understands an extrovert therapy dog is no substitute for human companionship. "Eventually, I'd like to meet someone whose poop I don't have to pick up. In the meantime, Tad has opened my eyes to new possibilities. It's hard to believe I've lived this long without chasing a squirrel."

Ask Mindy Menorah:

Twenty or More Is the Loneliest Number

Dear Mindy: Frank and I have been together for two years. We're your typical extrovert/introvert couple. He's gregarious. I can barely tolerate my cat who can't stop mewing to let me get a word in edgewise. I prefer to socialize with a few friends—by few, I mean in numbers from zero to Frank. Frank prefers rubbing shoulders with the Mormon Tabernacle Choir.

Last week I made reservations for two at a small, intimate restaurant. Frank invited a pack of cousins, five of whom belong to a *Deliverance* reenactors' club. I've never been a devotee of one-tooth banjo pickers, but I couldn't bring myself to say no.

This happens all the time. Frank always insists we socialize as part of a mob. (I'll save our evening with the Gagliano crime family for another question.) I love him dearly and want this relationship to work. How can I convince him to respect my need for solitude and shorter conga lines?
Mobbed in Manhasset

Dear Mobbed: Introvert/extrovert relationships can be a mixed blessing. I once dated an extrovert who wanted to have a three-way with me and my inner voice. This same extrovert introduced me to the amazing world of group rates.

A loving and thoughtful extrovert can help you emerge from your shell and broaden your world. But stand up for yourself. Just because you're not an extrovert doesn't mean you can't be an introvert princess warrior. Frank sounds like a keeper. Tell him how you feel, preferably not while doing the wave at a sports bar.

Mindy Menorah, Ph.D., LCSW, PDF *is a licensed, bonded, and bounded couples therapist. For twenty-three years she was the official Osmond family mediator.*

Variety is the Spice of Strife

Jump Start Your Introvert/ Extrovert Love Life

How do you rekindle the magic that made you ignore your obvious introvert/extrovert differences? Here are some suggestions.

If you are an introvert:

- Greet your extrovert at the door wearing nothing but your inner thoughts.

- Surprise your extrovert with a new sexual position where you're both in the same room.

- Talk dirty nonstop to your extrovert. Just avoiding unbearable silence will turn him on.

- Ask your extrovert if the voices in your head can watch.

If you are an extrovert:

- Dress up as an unapproachable French maid.

- Go to an introvert swap party, don't mingle, and leave after five minutes.

- Be more affectionate with your introvert. Don't say, "Why aren't you talking?" Say, "You really turn me on when you're uncommunicative."

- Call up your introvert partner for some hot phone sex and them let them get a word in edgewise.

Introverted Groom Hospitalized in Dancing Accident

Ellis McKinney was rushed to a local hospital shortly after he and his bride began the first dance at their wedding reception. The highly introverted groom lost consciousness after collapsing from self-consciousness.

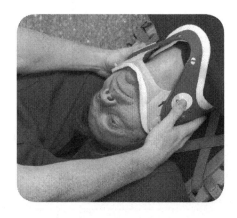

Seconds after the band launched into "Just in Time," McKinney noticed hundreds of partygoers watching him. He began to hyperventilate, spun around in what appeared to be a fancy dance move, and dizzily fell to the floor. Bride Janice Ankelman-McKinney started screaming hysterically after she realized he wasn't break dancing.

"He told me he felt extremely uneasy being the center of attention," sobbed Ankelman-McKinney. "I tried to make things easier for him. We had his identical twin brother fill in for him on the reception line."

Best man Neil Copper said, "I'm not surprised this happened. At our bachelor party, he kept telling the stripper giving him a lap dance, 'Please, I need my space.'"

Although still in shock, his young bride said she's relieved and "thankful I didn't ask him to do the Chicken Dance. It would've killed him."

McKinney regained consciousness in the hospital but became agitated when his nurse began humming "Sunrise Sunset." He's expected to fully recover.

Wife Catches Husband Cheating on Her with Himself

An Indiana wife confronted her husband after discovering he was involved with someone else: himself.

"I have to accept some of the blame," said Marcy Klein. "From the moment we met, I sensed he wanted to be alone but I ignored my instincts. I finally confronted him: 'What do you have that I don't?' He'd said I was crazy, that I was the only one. The fact that he never remembers my name should've been a tipoff."

After enduring his aloofness and almost total silence for three years, she was certain he was seeing another woman. Klein hired a private detective who tracked him to a nearby motel. Shortly thereafter, she confronted him with photos taken by the detective, pictures that clearly showed Harold in bed by himself reading a book.

When faced with the irrefutable evidence, Mr. Klein quickly confessed. He admitted he was an extreme introvert who'd been carrying on a lifelong relationship with himself. "I've never been able to say no to me," he sobbed.

Harold begged Marcy to give him another chance. He even gave her permission to cheat on him with herself to get back at him. She made reservations at a local bed and breakfast but couldn't go through with it.

He then suggested they see a marriage therapist who recommended the Kleins go on a double date with their inner selves. "I haven't been able to wrap my head around that concept," said Marcy "but I'm willing to give it a try for the sake of our marriage."

Oddly Happy Odd Couples

Are you skeptical about introvert/extrovert relationships? Let these couples set you straight.

Marshall: When we met, we didn't think we had a thing in common. Then we realized we both love small-time robberies and driving getaway cars.

Lisa: I won't lie, Marshall's long periods of silence sometimes bother me, but he more than compensates for it when he wakes up during the night screaming Italian arias.

Carmella: Romaine respects my need for my own space. Sometimes up to three inches apart.

Romaine: Carmella suggested we take separate vacations, so I agreed to five inches apart.

Francesca: It was tough when we first started dating. I wanted to go out and party at the senior center. He wanted to stay home and catalogue his spork collection.

Lionel: Francesca opened my eyes to new world. I'm still quiet and shy but have to admit I love going with her to clothing-optional bingo nights.

Siamese Introvert/Extrovert Twins Struggle to Get Along

Introvert/extrovert relationships often work because their differing personalities complement each other. This has not been the case for Chelsea and Simone Chesterfield, Siamese twin sisters.

"No matter how many times I say 'I need to be alone,' my sister just doesn't get it," says introvert Simone. "I hate to be a party pooper, but I hate parties. We can't even sit alone on the couch because Chelsea always wants to flirt and dance."

Extrovert Chelsea tries to be understanding, but it's frustrating. "I get it, she likes her solitude, but I need to socialize. I'm not asking Simone to double date. She can bring a book, or daydream, or whatever."

Simone says she's been accommodating. "Not to be too graphic, but after Chelsea has been drinking all night, guess which one of us gets sick and has the hangover? Last year, she signed us up for an ocean cruise, and I still haven't recovered from the limbo contest."

Chelsea defends herself. "If it weren't for me, Simone would have no idea what the outside world is like. Pulling four hamstrings in a limbo contest is a small price to pay for the opportunity to watch a beautiful Caribbean sunset."

"Yes," adds Simone. "Watching the sun set while I'm telling a drunken ship's mate he's got his tongue in the wrong ear."

"I understand our situation is unique," says Chelsea. "She's my sister, and I'd never leave her. But I can't change. To paraphrase Frank Sinatra, 'I've got to be us.'"

CHAPTER 11

Would You Be Happier as an Extrovert? Hint: Imagine a Chatty Three-Hour Group Hug

Do you ever wonder if the grass is greener on the more talkative side of the fence? It's only natural. Extroverts look like they're having so much fun—especially the ones who won't stop telling you how much fun they're having.

Are you considering a "conversion"? Most experts say it won't work, but why not give it a try? What's the worst that could happen—aside from ending up stranded at a Caribbean resort with 8,000 members of Back Slappers International? At the very least you'll have some fascinating stories to tell yourself.

Can You Fake Being an Extrovert?

Some experts believe introverts can fit better in extrovert situations by pretending to be extroverts. These experts also believe you can train a cocker spaniel to make a great cup of cappuccino.

If you still think acting like an extrovert will help get you through the day, get a promotion, or get to first base with Sally in software, here are some tips to guide you.

- Proper body language is key to being a good extrovert. Stand up straight and lean into conversations. Extroverts love to smell what the other person had for lunch.

- Gesture a lot, the broader the better. It may be hard at first. Pretend you're guiding a jet plane to the terminal.

- Smile. Extroverts are drawn to beaming faces. But be careful: A sudden transformation from sullen to euphoric data analyst can raise suspicions about psychoactive medication changes.

- Show you're genuinely interested in others. Ask people what they think. Tip: Don't walk away before they answer.

- Get people to talk about themselves. You'll feel more connected. However, a word of warning: This may lead to endless monologues about family reunion cruises to Staten Island and colonoscopy war stories. Keep your cell phone handy for a fake emergency call.

Remember, not every introvert can pretend to go both ways. But you'll never know until you dominate a conversation about a topic about which you know nothing.

Advice from Andy Brightman:
Monkey See, Monkey Needs His Space

Dear Andy: I'm an extreme introvert. How extreme? I've yet to introduce myself to my goldfish.

I was recently required to attend a cocktail party hosted by my employer. It was the kind of social gathering I avoid like a plague, the kind of plague in which I don't know the other plague victims.

To help survive the evening I enlisted the assistance of an amateur hypnotist friend who claimed he could transform me into an extrovert. Unfortunately, he thought it would be funny to transform me into an extroverted monkey every time someone said the word "strategize."

Aside from one small incident when I hurled my feces at the VP of sales, the evening went well. I even approached and flirted with our new intern from Uzbekistan. She speaks little English and found my outgoing simian airs enchanting. We've since been dating regularly for two months.

Here's my dilemma. Continuing to speak and act like a monkey hasn't been a problem. Continuing to speak and act like an extroverted monkey has. It takes so much energy and is exhausting. I like this girl and don't want to lose her. What do I do?

Going Bananas in Birmingham

Dear Bananas: There is nothing wrong with going ape for a girl, even a girl who can't tell the difference between a human and another mammal. But in the end, you have to listen to your inner primate. You're an introvert and will always be an introvert. Give your Uzbeki intern a chance. If she loves you as an outgoing monkey, she may come to appreciate you as a solitary, thoughtful chimpanzee.

Andy Brightman *is a former CIA intelligence officer.* To Hell and Back: My Thirty-Five Years in Cubicle 289D *is his recently published autobiography.*

Extroverted Like Me

What is it like to be an extrovert; to live each day with an insatiable need for social interaction; to speak before completing your thoughts; and to feel comfortable in large groups of people regardless of their taste in music?

I am an introvert and want to find out.

I must first prepare for my experiment. I need to learn how extroverts think and what they feel. I am sitting near the hostess stand at an Olive Garden restaurant, observing them smiling, making eye contact, and greeting each other warmly. Some even talk to strangers, using phrases like, "Hi there" and "Have you eaten here before?"

The day finally comes for me to assume my identity as an extrovert. I wake early, shower, and choose my wardrobe. For the first time in years I do not dress in black. For the first time in years I will leave my beret at home.

As is my normal routine, I eat breakfast while watching *BBC News: Bulgaria*. I finish my tea and turn the TV off. My pulse quickens. Slowly I stand up and prepare to leave the comfort and security of my 800-square-foot sanctuary and head into the extrovert world.

Two hours later I reach the outside of my apartment. I lock the door and turn around. Running directly at me is an Amazon deliveryman winding up to heave a package on my front step. I take a deep breath. Here goes nothing: "Hey, how ya doin'? Thanks so much, buddy! Have a great day!"

I stagger back into my apartment. It is worse than I thought.

Ten Signs Your Conversion from Introvert to Extrovert Isn't Working

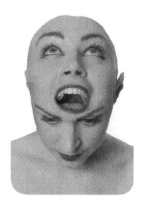

1. You're starting to avoid your new fifty-eight best friends.

2. You were rushed to an emergency room after collapsing while saying, "Nice weather we've been having."

3. You thought your TED Talk was going great until you realized you were talking to yourself.

4. You picked up a man up at a bar, took him back to your apartment, tore his clothes off, and told him you needed to be alone.

5. You only have the emotional energy at meetings to run ideas halfway up the flagpole.

6. You've developed a nervous tic every time you say "Sure, I'd love to come to your party!"

7. You miss people asking "Are you okay?"

8. You faint each time you say, "Sure, the more the merrier."

9. You keep thinking about the spontaneous things you're going to say.

10. This carefree joy crap is starting to wear you down.

CHAPTER 12

Why Johnny Can't Fist Bump

It's the worst news parents think they can receive: Nursery networking makes their child feel like a phony.

They should fear not. It isn't the end of the world. Many introverted children grow up to be introverted doctors, lawyers, artists, and billionaire recluses. Still more will buy their parents a retirement condo in Boca Raton.

The key is to keep the lines of communication open, and make sure their children don't legally change their names to Damian or Aurora until they're at least thirteen.

Pre-Life Is Just a Bowl of Cherries

What was the best time of your life—high school, college, your twenties, thirties, or forties?

Many introverts would go back to a womb of one's own.

Why?

- It's the only time you could relax without bracing for human inter-action—unless you were a twin or triplet.

- Life in the womb was the first and last time you were part of the "in" crowd, albeit a crowd of one.

- You could be unapproachable to your heart's content because no one approached you.

- There was no agonizing small talk. Not once did anyone ask, "Nice womb, who's your decorator?"

- No one asked, "Why are you so quiet?" Just as well since you didn't know how to speak.

In short, it was the most normal you would ever feel—until a doctor slapped you and tried to make small talk, saying "Welcome to the world."

Sesame Street Introduces New Introverted Character

Sesame Street is set to unveil its new introverted character, Solomo. "We thought it was time to address the large number of kids who prefer to spend time alone reading or playing by themselves rather than seeking companionship with other kids," explained a *Sesame Street* spokespuppet.

Solomo will encourage introverted children by:

- Showing the joys of being alone on a deserted rundown city street in a dimly lit neighborhood.

- Encouraging them to be kind and considerate to their imaginary friends.

- Explaining how to say in a nice way to extroverted *Sesame Street* characters: "I don't want to open up."

- Teaching basic math skills like counting the minutes until they are alone.

- Explaining to Kermit it's not easy being green, but it's also not easy listening to a frog croak nonstop about it.

In addition to being the first introverted character, Solomo will also be the first Muppet to shut his bedroom door so the camera doesn't invade his privacy.

Explaining Introversion to Your Parents

Being a kid is tough. Being a kid, whose parents are clueless about your introversion, is tougher.

Do you have trouble explaining your introversion to your parents? You need to tell your mom and dad how you feel. The following lines might help them understand.

- I never feel more alive than when I'm relaxing underneath my bed.

- I'd love to hear more about the birds and bees, but you're exhausting me.

- I'm not shy. Would a shy kid belong to a goth barbershop quartet?

- I'm fairly certain puberty makes you averse to sentences shorter than three words.

- Can I have fifty dollars for meditation camp?

- Disneyworld is okay. I just wish it had an It's a Solitary World After All ride.

- I'm not always quiet. I've been talking to myself for the past three months.

Growing Up in an Extrovert Family

Being the only introvert in an extrovert family is never easy—a problem that doesn't seem to improve even after turning twenty-eight and still living in your parents' basement.

Here are some helpful strategies that can improve your family relationships.

Set an interaction quota: Reward yourself each day for speaking to one of your siblings and ignoring the others—on a rotating basis, of course. If you hug one of them, take the rest of the year off.

Find your personal networking style: For a lot of kids, it's throwing food. For others, it's screaming for help after you've been stuffed into your toy chest by a playful sibling.

Work on your conversation-starters: Introverts like to plan conversations in their heads, sometimes for the next seventeen years. It never hurts to prepare lines like, "Dad, I got drunk and crashed the car." Or, "Mom, I charged a tattoo and a nose piercing to your credit card."

Find the other family introverts: Your self-absorption may have prevented you from noticing there are additional loners in the family. Do you have a sibling who built a tree house with a reading room?

Smile: But not so much your parents think you've joined a cult.

Concerned Teens Form Introvert-Extrovert Alliance

The Barbra Streisand Vocational High School in Pacific Palisades has formed an Introvert-Extrovert Alliance (IEA). The Alliance is a student-run club that brings together introverts and extroverts to support each other and provide a safe place to socialize.

Gail, the only introvert member of the organization so far, said she appreciates her extroverted classmates' concern. "I'd probably attend more meetings, or even one meeting, if it weren't for the twenty-minute greeting embraces."

Senior class president Phil Tyler came up with the idea for the Introvert-Extrovert Alliance. "I always felt bad for the quiet students who never went to parties or hung out with everyone else—particularly the ones I deemed worthy of being my friends."

So far, IEA has attracted more extroverts than introverts. "For some reason, our weekly dance parties aren't as popular with the introverts," said Tyler. "I'm not giving up. It's important we create a large, safe, and supportive environment for every teenager who wants to be left alone."

I Feel Pretty Drained

An Illinois high school has a found a novel way to stage the classic musical *West Side Story*, while avoiding ethnic stereotypes.

The drama club at Alphonse Capone High School in suburban Chicago is replacing the traditional Anglo and Puerto Rican gangs with introverts and extroverts.

"We thought this would make the play more relatable," said drama club faculty advisor Ramona Proscenium. "Who doesn't identify with the group of extroverts dancing across an alley while snapping fingers, or a group of brooding introverts sitting quietly by themselves contemplating violence at a big dance?"

Staging a musical with introvert and extrovert street gangs has not been without challenges. For example, the introvert gang appears together throughout the show, but only for short periods of time. Said Devin Harris who plays Tony, "My character can take only so much socialization. That's why he sings most of his songs while reading a book in his bedroom." The rest of the introvert gang spends much of the show offstage, trying not to be noticed.

The show's most complex character is Maria, an ambivert* portrayed by Lucy Spitsink. "I have a dual personality. One moment I'm singing to myself in front of a mirror. The next moment I'm trying not to notice myself in front of a mirror." The toughest part, she says, is singing duets with Tony, since "he's always on the other side of town in his bedroom reading a book. But that's the magic of theater."

*Ambivert: Someone who exhibits both introvert and extrovert characteristics. Think bisexual with half the fun.

CHAPTER 13

I'm Not an Animal, I'm an Introvert: Explaining Yourself to the Extrovert World

We introverts have all been there before: We're minding our own business with a dead expression on our face when someone asks, "Should I call an ambulance?"

Here we go again.

Trying to explain yourself to extroverts is like explaining infinity to a monkey. They say they understand, but five minutes later they want to throw a banana at you.

Still, we keep trying to make ourselves understood, preferably from a safe distance via a text message.

In the end, there are two types of non-introverts: those who understand who you are and those who keep interrupting you while you're trying to explain who you are.

Debutante Ball Presents Introvert Women to Extrovert Society

Daughters of the world's crème de la reticent reluctantly presented themselves to high society at a glittering debutante ball in New York City.

Here is a partial list of this year's introvert debutante coterie.

Felicity Searing Saltonstall is entering her twelfth year and thirty-second major at Hampshire College where she is currently studying the label on a maple syrup bottle. Active in Habitat for Hummus, she is vice president and sole member of her book discussion group.

She is the daughter of Mr. and Mrs. Dwight Pepper Saltonstall. Pending final hormone treatments, her mother is the former Frank Peabody.

Doris Drysdale Flotsam has been homeschooled by four stepmothers and three life partners. She is currently working on her doctoral thesis, "The Effects of Breastfeeding While Playing Tennis." She plans to study abroad next year in her neighbor's attic.

She is the daughter of Mr. Fenwick Dillinger Flotsam and either Mrs. Judith Epstein Bordon or a hitchhiker who claimed to be Patty Hearst's sister.

Nora Rayford Doodlehauf is a junior at Bennington College where she majors in journaling and minors in alienation. She spent last summer teaching an isolated Amazon tribe how to feel even more isolated.

Nora enjoys writing 1000-word Post-it notes reminding people to be more considerate and waiting until her roommate leaves for the weekend so she can breathe.

She is the daughter of Mr. and Mrs. Sheldon Hatfield Doodlehauf III, her mother the former Margo Zinnia Rampick.

Confessions of an Introverted Santa

The first time a kid sat on my lap, all I could think was "I need a cigarette." And I don't smoke.

I know I scare children. I try to connect with them, but they just don't see the real me.

I never smile or look directly at the children. That doesn't mean I'm unfriendly. Why can't they understand that? If they took some time and got to know me, rather than running in tears to their parents, they'd realize I'm a decent Santa.

This is not an easy job. The small talk is brutal: "Have you been good girl this year?" "What do you want Santa to bring you for Christmas?" What I really want to ask is: "Are you adopted?" "Do you have ADD?" "Is your mother divorced?" "Is she dating?" "Do you think she'd have a drink with me?"

The few kids I don't scare off talk to me like I'm their friend, but they don't really know me. To them I'm a jolly old man from the North Pole. There's so much more to me than that.

Yes, it's nice to bring joy to their lives, but it would be also nice to have an intelligent conversation about child labor exploitation in Bangladesh.

Don't get me wrong. I'm not a total pessimist. I still believe in the miracle of Christmas and the goodness of man. And I believe that one day an adorable little child will jump up on my lap and say, "Santa, I get you."

Good Samaritan Becomes Despondent Trying to Cheer Up Introverts

MARK LOOFTON

Last year, I joined the Do a Good Deed or Die Doing It Club. I pledged to brighten up every introvert I know—whether they liked it or not.

So far, I'm batting zero and totally depressed. Introverts are now approaching *me* and asking, "Are you okay?"

Each time I try to console an introvert friend in need, their reaction is always the same:

"I am happy."

"Just because I'm not smiling doesn't mean there's something wrong."

"Did you *not* read the restraining order?"

I wish I could convince my socially averse friends that being more approachable brings immeasurable joy into their lives. If only they knew the pleasure I feel each time a coworker I vaguely know approaches me and proceeds to talk nonstop about her psoriasis.

I understand, a perpetual grim facial expression has its advantages. For example, you always look like your driver's license photo. And yes, there is something sexy about clenched teeth and a guttural growl.

But I can't believe introverts with gloomy demeanors are really happy—especially the ones who see me approaching.

Mark Loofton *is a door-to-door doorbell salesman. He holds the Guinness World Record for the longest period of time without taking no for an answer.*

CHAPTER 14

Some Introverts Are Born Great, All Are Great at Avoiding Loud Award Ceremonies

Many famous people have been and are introverts. For example, Alexander The Great preferred being called Alex because it brought less attention to himself. Thomas Edison invented the lightbulb so that it would be easier for him to read alone in his food pantry.

Being an introvert allows you to focus on doing great things. Did you know Sir Isaac Newton, the man who formulated the laws of motion and universal gravitation, also invented the first foldable Do Not Disturb sign?

Famous introverts are inspiring. Just knowing that Lady Gaga is an introvert has inspired a generation of introverts to say, "Really? I can do better than that."

You may never have Abraham Lincoln's resume, but that doesn't mean you can't study hard in school and grow up to be an expert rail splitter.

Take inspiration from these great introverts. Also, try not to focus on the famous loners who've gone on to do unspeakable things. Caligula had issues that had nothing to do with being an introvert.

Profiles in Introversion: Johnny Appleseed

Johnny Appleseed (born John Chapman, September 26, 1774–March 11, 1845) was an American pioneer who introduced the country to apple trees and the introvert lifestyle.

Although legend paints a picture of Johnny wandering the countryside planting apple trees, he did much more. He introduced early America to a brooding behavior that would change and annoy the nation forever.

Beginning in 1792, Johnny headed west to plant apple trees and be alone. Today, Native Americans from the Iroquois tribe in New York tell the story of a man they call Scatchwhoa (translation: man who dislikes small talk).

After growing bored with the Iroquois, Johnny moved to Pennsylvania. He continued traveling into the Ohio Valley country and Indiana. Each year he planted apple seeds for settlers who would've been more grateful had he not seemed so aloof and conceited.

Johnny—soon known as the "apple seed man"—always carried a leather bag filled with apple seeds, making him the first American to sport a man purse. Legend has it that some of the locals dubbed him "metrosexual apple seed man."

Johnny Appleseed never married. He did have a long, intense relationship with a woman known as Patricia Peach Pit. In the end, it was not meant to be. "We tried to make the relationship work," Johnny wrote to his brother. "But we're apples and peaches. And she's not interested in being just a cross-pollination buddy."

Johnny died peacefully on March 18, 1845, having made the fledgling country apple-friendly and more open to eccentric guys living by themselves in the woods.

Greatest Quotes by Famous Film Introverts Left on the Cutting Room Floor

Rick Blaine *(Casablanca)*: Here's not looking at you, kid.

Travis Bickle *(Taxi Driver)*: You talkin' to me? If so, you're boring the hell out of me.

Terry Malloy *(On the Waterfront)*: I coulda been a contender. But I'm horrible in job interviews.

Scarlett O'Hara *(Gone with the Wind)*: As God is my witness, I will never have three roommates again.

Cole Sear *(The Sixth Sense)*: I see dead people and they're asking me about the weather.

Harry Callahan *(Dirty Harry)*: Go ahead, make my day. Tell me the chief's retirement party isn't mandatory.

George M. Cohan *(Yankee Doodle Dandy)*: My mother thanks you. My father thanks you. My sister thanks you. And I thank you. Begorra, I need to decompress.

Lou Gehrig *(The Pride of the Yankees)*: I consider myself the luckiest man on the face of the earth. I'd be luckier if I could deliver this speech from my apartment.

Dorothy *(The Wizard of Oz)*: There's no place like home alone with a good book.

Jennifer Cavilleri Barrett *(Love Story)*: Love means never having to say, "Please, I need my own space."

Marcel Marceau's Confined Quotient of Quietness

You would think having a job that requires being silent would be the perfect occupation for an introvert. Marcel Marceau (1923–2007), universally considered the world's greatest mime, thought otherwise.

He was a classic introvert. At gatherings, he hated small mime. It was practically impossible for him to gesture, "How are you?" "Nice tie, where did you buy it?" or "You must give me the recipe for these invisible cheese puffs!"

Marceau told his imaginary biographer, "I can put myself in invisible rooms, but I can't keep invisible people out. I try to ignore them. They always want to say. 'Hello,' ask how I'm doing, and sell me pretend life insurance."

He spent his life trying to avoid imaginary people. "On an intellectual level I know they don't exist, but I can't avoid them," Marceau told a reporter from *Popular Mime* magazine in 1977. He revealed in the same interview he'd been seeing an invisible therapist for the past twenty-five years. "Sure, I could make more progress with an actual therapist, but my guy charges so little and he really understands me."

Marcel Marceau was married three times, once to a woman who actually existed. "It was always the same problem: 'Marcel, why are you so quiet?' 'Marcel, stop smelling that invisible flower and come to bed.' I've always preferred one-on-none relationships. But every time I create an invisible wall to keep the world out, I allow another beautiful invisible creature back in my heart. I'm the classic introvert. I can't live with imaginary people. I can't live without them."

7 Interesting Facts about the Loch Ness Introvert

1. She lives by herself in Loch Ness in the Scottish Highlands.

2. There's nothing she hates more than meeting new monsters.

3. If you really want to make the Loch Ness Introvert angry, throw her a surprise birthday party.

4. She's been spotted more frequently since she started dating the Loch Ness Extrovert.

5. If you spot the Loch Ness Introvert by herself reading a book, steer clear; it's a passive-aggressive indication she wants to be alone.

6. She does have a small group of close monster friends, and she's a good listener.

7. The BBC is planning a miniseries about The Loch Ness Introvert. She will be played by Dame Judi Dench.

Look Away, I Have Something to Say

Eminent introverts have faced the terrifying gaze of adoring crowds. How some have dealt with this personal nightmare can provide insight for all introverts.

Albert Einstein: Whenever I get nervous about an audience looking at me, I immediately explain my theory of relativity in detail. Within seconds, most of them doze off.

Abraham Lincoln: During the first Me-Douglas debate, I tried to overcome my anxieties by imagining everyone in the audience was naked. It was working until a very heavy and hairy gentleman sat down in the front row. I became nauseated during my Martin Van Buren impersonation and lost my train of thought. What relaxes me now is imagining I'm alone in a log cabin, binge-reading Shakespeare.

Eleanor Roosevelt: I've always been nervous in large crowds—particularly Roosevelt family reunions. But my Uncle Teddy gave me the greatest advice: "Speak softly and maybe people won't notice you."

Mahatma Gandhi: It's a lot easier to fast alone when the alternative is sitting in a crowded restaurant with strangers looking at me and thinking, "He should fast. He could lose a few pounds."

Charles Darwin: I used to wonder why hating people looking at me didn't kill me. Then I came up with this theory about introverts called Survival of the Moodiest.

Jimi Hendrix: People are looking at me? Man, I thought those were gerbils.

Great Moments in Introvert History: Houdini Escapes Cocktail Party

On June 28, 1921, illusionist, escape artist, and introvert Harry Houdini attended a party of potential investors for his next show. Within minutes after arriving, Houdini was adrift in an ocean of adoring eyeballs. His devoted fans asked questions impossible for any antisocial escapologist to answer: "How are you tonight?" "Is this your lovely wife?" "Nice straitjacket. How much did you pay for it?"

Houdini began to panic. He was packed in a crowd of strangers twenty deep and needed desperately to be alone. No introvert trapped by a mass of people this large had ever escaped. The few people who sensed his discomfort that evening believed the great Houdini had finally met his match . . . until a waiter dropped a tray of crab cakes.

Without being noticed, Houdini slipped silently to the floor and slithered to the bathroom, where he spent the next two hours alphabetizing the contents of the medicine cabinet.

After three hours, a partygoer, who'd become violently ill after eating some dirty crab cakes, pounded violently on the bathroom door. Houdini dropped the magazine he'd been reading and jumped through a small second-story window. He rolled off the front sidewalk and limped to a local hospital, where he was treated for dog bites and a broken ankle.

After sending his hosts a thank-you note, Harry Houdini went on to become one of the greatest escape artists of all time. He is also an inspiration for every introvert who has ever thought, "One way or another I have to flee this party."

CHAPTER 15

You'll Always Walk Alone: Being at One with Your One Self

You know you are an introvert. But are you comfortable being an introvert? Not sure? Ask yourself three questions.

1. Do you find the words, "For the last time, come out of your room" soothing?

2. In meetings, do you enjoy reading a newspaper while your fellow Joint Chiefs of Staff jabber away?

3. Do you find an aloof grimace across a candlelit table arousing?

If you answered yes to any of these questions, you may cancel the rest of your therapy appointments. Go directly to the beach and enjoy a sunset free of charge.

All We Are Saying Is Give Introversion a Chance

Did you ever wonder what it would be like if everyone was an introvert?

- Everybody could feel alone together.

- No more small talk. Simple greetings would last for days.

- On the slim chance people came to a party and they didn't know each other, it would be considered good manners to silently grab something to eat and leave.

- All classroom seats would be located at the back of the room where everyone could avoid being noticed.

- As a precaution, designated introverts would be assigned to call other introverts and say, "You haven't left your apartment since 2009. Let's go out and throw the Frisbee."

- Successful job candidates would be hired based on being unapproachable and staring down at the interviewer's shoes.

- The phrase "the more the merrier" would be outlawed.

I've Been A Very Bad Introvert

Larry, a bookstore manager from San Francisco, is an extreme introvert who prefers quiet evenings in his apartment alone reading and playing his recorder.

However, Larry (not his real name) has another life. He occasionally likes to explore a darker side of his introversion with the help of a dominatrix, Mistress Shtum.

"It took a long time for me to admit," says Larry, "that there's another side to me who enjoys being punished for being quiet. I experimented with other dominatrices, most of who were truly annoyed by my silent nature. They usually offered to punish me free of charge. Mistress Shtum understands me and my limits. As strange as it sounds, she's the only person I feel safe with while being hogtied for not being more talkative."

Mistress Shtum (her real name) specializes in introverted submissive fetishes. She says her introverted clients have particularly vivid fantasies. It can be anything, from being ordered to attend a crowded Tupperware party wearing a nickel-plated thong, to being strapped in a barber's chair while talking on the phone for hours with a distant relative.

"I help my slaves explore their fears and desires. Ordering someone to hand out their business cards at a networking conference may sound cruel, but they trust me. I never have them engage in small talk with a Verizon salesperson without first agreeing to a safe word—actually a safe paragraph."

"This lifestyle isn't for all introverts," says Larry. "There was a time in my life when the thought of being handcuffed to a talkative former cheerleader while trying to read a book would've repulsed me. I now understand there's nothing more liberating than being totally humiliated and degraded—as long as it's followed with lots of quiet time."

Live Like a Billionaire Hermit on a Budget

Do you seek the solitary life of a reclusive billionaire or James Bond villain, but lack the resources to buy a tropical island or build an army of bikini-clad robot security guards?

Even if you calculate your net worth in nickels and dimes, you can still live like a mad ruler of an isolated empire. Simply follow these easy steps.

Reconfigure your living space: With some creative decorating, you can make any studio apartment feel like a walled-off fortress in the Himalayas. Go heavy on the earth tones and add an audio loop of angry, exotic birds mating.

Stock twenty-five years of supplies: Plan carefully. For example, how will you feel about Dinty Moore Beef Stew after the 10,000th can?

Declare yourself ruler of your domain: Publish your manifesto on Facebook, along with a photo of you wearing a crown and holding a scepter. Note: Make sure your *Breakfast Club* poster is not in the background.

Security is essential: If your condo community forbids alligator-filled moats, consider hiring a retired lizard to patrol your foyer.

A minimum amount of companionship is essential: Mechanical spouses or motorized significant others can be cost-prohibitive. However, retrofitting an inflatable doll is a less expensive alternative. They are great listeners, tolerable lovers, and never make demands on you.

Stay in touch with family and friends: Just because you're off the grid doesn't mean you can't attend Thanksgiving dinners, family reunions, and funerals via Skype.

Remember, introverts are incredible dreamers, a quality that enables them to accomplish practically anything in their minds. You may not live in a 100-story skyscraper surrounded by barbed wire on a tropical island. It doesn't mean you can't run a toenail-clipping recycling conglomerate from the comfort of your breakfast nook.

Join the Subdued Revolution! (Exclamation Point Optional)

Introverts of the world (or at least the ones reading this book): For too long we have been marginalized by a society that values talkative, engaging people with competent social skills.

It is time we collectively rise up and say under our breaths, "No More!"

Together we can show the world that introverts are more than quiet people who prefer to stay at home and read a book. We also like to stay at home and watch TV, write in our journals, and defrost our refrigerators.

Movements that change the world often begin with mass rallies designed to excite and motivate followers. Since large gatherings are the last place introverts want to be, let's recite from the privacy of our homes the Silent Revolution Declaration of Purpose:

If I see something, I will say nothing (for reasons altogether different from the Mafia Declaration of Purpose).

If a friend wants to know if I'm interested in going to a party, I will screen her phone call and not answer it.

Whenever I am in a diner or park reading and someone asks, "Is that a good book?" I will act as though I can't hear them.

At work, I will always pretend I'm taking an important phone call so no one bothers me.

If someone still insists on bothering me while I'm pretending to take an important phone call, I will ask the pretend caller, "How much longer does he have to live?"

Whenever someone asks, "Why are you so quiet?" I will try not to scream, "Because I have nothing to say!"—but I won't try very hard.

Regrets, We Don't Need No Stink'n Regrets

Do you feel being an introvert has caused you to miss good opportunities in life?

Really? Think about the bad ones you've avoided.

- You weren't popular in high school. But you didn't marry Bunny the head cheerleader who now weighs 250 pounds and travels the child beauty pageant circuit with her Honey Boo Boo-ish daughter.

- Your less-than-firm handshake may have cost you the CEO job at your hedge fund company. It may have also saved you from an SEC indictment.

- With a few more connections you might've found a famous film director to read your screenplay. At least you didn't have to deal with rejection when Arnold Schwarzenegger passed on *Conan the Technical Writer*.

- You've always struggled with job interviews. In the long run, however, it forced you to pursue your real dream: freelance maracas player.

- It's been hard to meet men because they think you're aloof and unapproachable. Luckily, these qualities have made you the most popular nymphomaniac at your Sexaholics Anonymous meetings.

- Your quietness makes people feel uncomfortable. It still comes in handy when people misinterpret your silence for wisdom.

So maybe your life would be different if you were more sociable. But better? What could be better than sitting alone contemplating if it could be better?

Acknowledgements

Susan Shulman saw a book when others saw a comical cry for help.

Bill Bowers and Joyce Alper showed ~~yours truly myself~~ me the importance of having good editors.

Lucy Bartholomay, a fellow mind traveler, beautifully melded printed words with images.

Anne Shuhler and Ivan Bolivar expertly translated my "design" concepts into a book that is readable by most earthlings.

Alma Alper taught and showed her "glorious mob" that "humor is important."

Myles Alper, the greatest fan a son could have

My big loving family always lets me sit and drink it all in.

My wife Monica, whose heart is as beautiful as her prose. She's my window to the outside world.

Advice, Inspiration and an Occasional Wince – Lauren Baratz-Logsted, Mary Bisbee-Beek, Callie Crossley, Sheila Cunningham, Patrick Dowdall, Susanne Dowdall, Myrtle Figueiredo, Bev Ford, Matthew Gilbert, Sandy Goroff, Mike Joroff, Lawrence Kessenich, Jacki Kronenberg, David Lennon, Stephanie Schorow, Jeannie Williams, Ande Zellman

Made in the USA
Middletown, DE
16 June 2019